Thinking about Death

edited by Peter Cave and Brendan Larvor

for the

Humanist Philosophers' Group

GW00703214

British Humanist Association
1 Gower Street
London WC1E 6HD

2004

ISBN 0 901825 23 9

Printed by Lavenham Press Ltd, Lavenham, Suffolk

Contributors

Piers Benn is Lecturer in Medical Ethics at Imperial College London. His doctoral thesis was on the nature and significance of death. He is the author of *Ethics*, and has published on ethics, applied ethics, philosophy of religion, and philosophical aspects of time and tense. He appears in the media from time to time.

Peter Cave is Associate Lecturer in Philosophy at The Open University and City University London and is the author of a wide range of articles, his most recent being 'Humour and Paradox Laid Bare', *The Monist*, **88.1** (2005) and 'Reeling and A-Reasoning', *Philosophy*, 79 (2004).

Anthony Flew, retired Professor of Philosophy, is the author of many books and articles, including *God and Philosophy*, *The Presumption of Atheism*, *Crime or Disease?*, *A Rational Animal: Philosophical Essays on the Nature of Man*, *The Logic of Mortality*, *Power to the Parents: Reversing Educational Decline*, *Atheistic Humanism*, *Social Life and Moral Judgment*.

John Harris holds the Sir David Alliance Chair of Bioethics at the University of Manchester and is the author of many papers and books, including *Clones, Genes and Immortality* (OUP 1998).

Brendan Larvor is Senior Lecturer in Philosophy at the University of Hertfordshire.

Tim LeBon is a practising philosophical counsellor and author of *Wise Therapy*. He is also co-editor of *Practical Philosophy* and an active member of the Society for Philosophy in Practice.

Hugh Mellor is Emeritus Professor of Philosophy and Fellow of Darwin College in the University of Cambridge. He is also a Fellow of the British Academy and of the Australian Academy of the Humanities, and chairman of the Analysis Trust. He is author of many books and articles on metaphysics, including *The Matter of Chance, Matters of Metaphysics, The Facts of Causation* and *Real Time II*.

Adam Smith (1723 – 1790), was a Scottish political economist and philosopher, who in 1776 wrote his most influential book, *The Wealth of Nations*.

Richard Swinburne is a Fellow of the British Academy, and was Nolloth Professor of the Philosophy of the Christian Religion, University of Oxford until 2002. He has written many books on the meaning and justification of the central claims of the Christian religion, the best known of which is *The Existence of God*, and on other philosophical issues, including *Epistemic Justification* and *The Evolution of the Soul*. The latter contains a full-length presentation of the ideas in his article in this book.

Suzanne Uniacke is Reader in Applied Ethics at the University of Hull. She has published widely in ethics, applied ethics and philosophy of law, including *Permissible Killing: The Self-Defence Justification of Homicide*.

Nigel Warburton is Senior Lecturer in Philosophy at the Open University and author of many books, including *Philosophy: the Basics; Philosophy: the Classics; Thinking from A to Z; The Art Question*; and a biography of architect Erno Goldfinger.

Acknowledgements

This book is based on a Humanist Philosophers' Group conference on death and dying, *Death: a Live Issue*, organised by the British Humanist Association and held on 19th October 2002 at Kings College, London. Many of the articles were specially written for the conference or this book and have not been published before; others, although published elsewhere and not written for the conference, are included because of their relevance to the theme.

The British Humanist Association is very grateful to the speakers at the conference and other contributors to this collection, and to the editors, all of whom freely and generously donated their time and articles.

Peter Cave's *Dead People* is a slightly revised version of a paper first published in *Think* 5 (Royal Institute of Philosophy, 2003), and his *Voluntary Sex* is a more radically revised version of a paper first published in *Philosophy Now*, 17 (1997). John Harris's *Intimations of Immortality* was first published in *Science Magazine* (Volume 288, Number 5463, 7 April 2000). Tim LeBon's *Six Months to Live* was first published in *Humanity,* Feb-Mar 2000 (BHA) and an adapted version appeared in *Wise Therapy* (Sage, 2001). Nigel Warburton's *The Gambler's Argument* was published in *Think*, Issue 7, Summer 2004.

Contents

Introduction

Peter Cave and Brendan Larvor

This collection of essays is intended to have a wide appeal. Dying and death affect all of us indirectly – and ultimately, of course, directly. We read of the deaths of millions of persons unknown to us, and we can become distressed; yet typically we are more intimately touched by those deaths much closer to home – deaths involving our family, friends and finally ourselves. We believe that the essays here will interest general readers as well as academics, religious believers as well as humanists and casual 'flickers-through' as well as payers of sustained attention.

The essays are diverse. In substance they range from the rights and wrongs of euthanasia to the possibility of an afterlife; from counselling someone with just a few months of remaining life to questioning whether a dead person can be harmed; and from the consequences of an earthly immortality to whether someone's death is a loss to that person. In form the essays are also diverse – ranging from traditional continuous prose articles to questions and answers and fictional dialogue.

The first four essays look at dying. A gut feeling might be that we should usually prefer not to die or, at least, would prefer to live for much, much longer – and increased years are indeed becoming more and more likely for those in the future with access to the best medical care. However, such extended longevity has social consequences. These are discussed in John Harris's *Intimations of Mortality*. Harris asks what will happen when it becomes possible to repair the effects of aging and chronic disease using cloned embryonic cells, growth factors or genetic therapies. He contends that these technologies could make many people virtually immortal (though not invulnerable to accidents and acute diseases). If a significant proportion of the population is quasi-immortal in this way, then either the population will rise until checked by scarce resources, or the birth rate will drop at least to match the reduced death rate. The first case is clearly undesirable. In the second case, suggests Harris, society could miss the vitality currently supplied by the young.

Suppose that the quasi-immortality outlined by Harris presented such social or economic problems. Is there any reason to suppose that they would be self-correcting in a benign way? If not, how could the resultant problems be addressed without violating some of the rights and values that we currently hold? Harris suggests that something – either our right to reproduce as we wish or our right to use all available medical trechnology to prolong our lives – would have to give way.

In addition to curing previously intractable conditions, advances in medical technology give us information that we might not otherwise have had. How is one to cope, for example, with the knowledge that one has about six months left to live? Philosophical counsellors use a mixture of philosophical techniques and traditional counselling to help with predicaments of this sort. Tim LeBon, in *Six Months to Live,* explains what philosophical counselling might have to offer someone in this situation.

Ever-improving medical technology enables people to survive conditions that would previously have killed them, yet that technology often fails to overcome the survivor's pain or debility. Consequently, there are more and more people wanting or needing, at the very least, to consider euthanasia. Their circumstances are such that, in practice, death appears preferable to more life. Incurable suffering, aged loneliness and an inability to get around – one's world shrinks – can lead some perfectly rational individuals to prefer quite simply to be dead rather than alive. Circumstances, though, might well mean that these individuals are unable to take their own lives; and so the plea for euthanasia comes to the fore. When the plea is voluntary, and someone kills that person or deliberately lets him die in that person's interests, philosophers usually speak of 'voluntary euthanasia'. Involuntary euthanasia occurs when a death is brought about in that person's interests yet against his wishes; and non-voluntary euthanasia occurs when the person expresses no wish either way, perhaps because he is in a persistent vegetative state.

It is often argued that voluntary euthanasia should not be permitted, because if it is permitted, we shall slide down a slippery slope and find ourselves acquiescing in non-voluntary euthanasia to varying degrees: there might be pressure on the elderly to accept euthanasia; there might develop a more casual attitude towards killing, even if not in that person's interests. Peter Cave's *Voluntary Sex* is a satire on this reasoning. It aims to stimulate debate over quite what sort of slope might specially apply in the case of killing but not in that of having sex. If no special reasons can be given for thinking the slope particularly applies in the euthanasia case, then there is no more reason to prohibit it than to prohibit consensual sex or, indeed, consensual flower arranging.

Euthanasia continues, though, to be illegal in the UK, yet suicide is no longer. Campaigners for the right to voluntary euthanasia may be tempted to argue that since suicide is legal, it should not be illegal to assist a suicide and so should not be illegal to engage in voluntary euthanasia. How (runs the thought) could it be reasonable to prosecute someone for helping somebody else to perform what would be a legal act if performed solely by that someone else? Suzanne Uniacke's *A Right to Die?* takes up this important question.

One should first note that the fact that suicide is legal does not entail that it is always morally unproblematic; so any argument in favour of euthanasia using the permissibility of suicide would need to draw on the moral permissibility of suicide, not its legal permissibility. Uniacke's response to the idea that voluntary euthanasia should be seen as assisted suicide, though, directly attacks the idea at the level of legal rights. Just because suicide is a legal right, we cannot argue that therefore voluntary euthanasia should be a legal right. For one simple thing, euthanasia demands the cooperation of someone other than the person wanting to die. Further, euthanasia is significantly different from suicide, Uniacke claims, because it aims to relieve the physical condition of the patient; it is therefore subject to the ethical and legal norms proper to medicine. If we forget this, we shall produce bad argument and bad law. In other words, if there is a case for legalising voluntary euthanasia, it must be because such mercy killing is *euthanasia*, and not merely because it is voluntary, though we need, of course, further investigation into the claimed linkage between euthanasia and medical practice.

'Call no man happy 'til he be dead' is a saying ascribed to the Athenian lawgiver, Solon. Only when we see the whole story of a person's life can we judge whether it went well. However, there may be significant biographical events after a person's death and so we might wonder whether, in some way, they might affect that person who lived. For example, it is part of the story of Oliver Cromwell that some years after his death his corpse was exhumed and decapitated, and his head displayed on a pole as that of a traitor. This was, no doubt, hurtful to his surviving friends and relatives, and it was damaging to his reputation, but did it harm Cromwell? Logically, it seems the answer is 'No': at that time Cromwell no longer existed, or if he did exist it was as a soul or spirit. In either case it was not Cromwell who was decapitated, but merely his corpse. However, this view would seem to make a mystery of our treatment of corpses. Funerals, it is sometimes said, are for the living, yet the bodies of people who leave no known friends or relatives are still usually treated respectfully; certainly, most people think that they should be treated respectfully. How can we make sense of this? These questions are considered in the next two essays of the collection. Both essayists, for the sake of the argument, assume death to be annihilation, thus avoiding claims that maybe eternal souls or spirits might be upset by what happens on earth.

In the first of these two essays, *How Should We Treat the Dead?*, Piers Benn notes that we can be harmed without knowing it (by secret slander or broken promises, for example). Therefore, the fact that dead people are unaware of damage to their bodies, or gravestones, or reputations, does not by itself show that there is no harm done to the person. Moreover, if the dead cannot be harmed, then they cannot be harmed by death, yet we know that death is, usually, a bad thing. If we have already decided that the dead cannot be harmed, then the badness of death cannot lie in the harm it does to the dead person. So if we insist that the dead cannot be harmed, we seem to make a mystery of the badness of death itself. Benn suggests that the badness of death is not any property of the predicament of being dead. Rather, the badness of death lies in the finitude of life; but, granting this, this does not answer the question of whether the dead can be harmed, once dead. Benn believes that they can be harmed; he suggests that this is so because our interests exist timelessly and therefore do not cease to exist when we die. This is an elegant solution, though it seems to suggest that our interests existed before we were born or even conceived which could lead us into the question of harms being done to us thousands of years before we were born. Also, some of our interests do have time limits. For example, after I die I want those who miss me to grieve no more or less than is proper and healthy. I do not want my friends and family to be indifferent to my passing, but nor I do not want them to be permanently paralysed by grief. This interest of mine persists after my death, but not after the death of the last person who knew me.

Peter Cave, in *Dead People*, starts the argument from a different place; he puts forwards a very simple argument, at least on the surface, namely that we should treat people well; therefore (*a fortiori*) we should treat dead people well. He considers and rejects thirteen objections to this argument. His crucial claim is that we are not separable from our projects and interests in the way that we would have to be if the dead were beyond harm. To kick my shin is to kick me; to damage my reputation is to damage me; to thwart my projects is to thwart me. Consequently, damage to my reputation or projects after my death is still damage inflicted against me. This, presumably, was the view of the vengeful monarchists – it was Cromwell they wanted to punish for treason, rather than his body or reputation. Nevertheless, we might wonder whether the body-parts, reputation and interests still add up to a person after death. Perhaps these elements form an intimate unity only in the living. Cromwell's head was exhibited on a spike, but we would not say that Cromwell was exhibited on a spike. If the royalists could exhibit Cromwell's head without exhibiting Cromwell, then perhaps they could harm Cromwell's reputation without harming Cromwell. However, were that thought sufficient to undermine Cave's position, we might equally well argue that, as we can shake our living Prime Minister's hand, conceal his toes and admire the strength of his argument, without, respectively, shaking, concealing and admiring him, then perhaps, because of such facts, we can also harm his reputation without harming him; yet that would be a paradoxical conclusion concerning someone living. Before any firm answers can be reached about such matters, we clearly need to know better quite what it is to be a person.

Death is universal, but the meaning of death is not. Attitudes to death change over the centuries. For example, previous generations would have been shocked at the suggestion that there is no afterlife, because without one there could be no guarantee of justice. In this life people rarely seem to get what they deserve. If the wicked are not punished and the virtuous rewarded after death, then, it might seem, we must reconcile ourselves to a morally indifferent universe. None of the three essays to which we now turn, on the possibility of an afterlife, considers the question of justice. It would appear that the moral indifference of the universe is no longer inconceivable or even shocking to most people. A prior question is, of course, that of what sense can be made of an afterlife; it is to this question in particular that the final group of essays turns.

The first of this group, *The Possibility of Life after Death*, is by a Christian, Richard Swinburne. Swinburne argues that a living human consists of a mortal body and an immortal soul. The immortal soul is the essential part of the person; it is the part that in some way carries one's personal identity. Since this soul continues to exist after it is separated from the body at death, it is proper to say that we continue to exist after our deaths. Swinburne argues this with a thought-experiment. Imagine that a mad surgeon were to divide your brain in half and implant each half in a different body. Which of these two individuals would then be you? One of them must be you, according to Swinburne, but there is no physical fact that decides the matter. So there must be something immaterial that settles it, and this is the soul. The soul would go with one of the bodies, and that body-plus-soul combination would be you. Swinburne's main claim is simply that there must be an immaterial soul, otherwise the identity question would be undecidable. He thus assumes that there must be a fact of the matter here.

Hugh Mellor in his *Reply* rejects Swinburne's argument. There is, he says, no reason to think that one of the bodies bearing half of your brain would have to be you and the other not. Suppose that the planet Venus were to split in half, resulting in two planets. It would make no sense to insist that one half must be the real Venus, numerically identical with the planet before the split, while the other is not. The question 'Which of these is the real Venus?' would simply have no answer. Similarly, there is no answer to Swinburne's demand to know which of the two bodies carrying half of your brain would be the real you. So there is no need to posit a soul to decide the matter. Therefore Swinburne's thought-experiment does not establish what he really needs for an afterlife, which is the possibility of a disembodied existence. In fact, Swinburne's attention to the brain in his argument encourages the thought that a disembodied existence is impossible. We should recall, though, that Swinburne was addressing a humanist gathering, and may have been seeking premises acceptable to his audience.

Both the question of an afterlife and the treatment of the dead lead quickly from universal human concerns and fears into some technical metaphysics. To know whether dead people might be harmed, we must raise the question again of what it is to be a person. The issue between Swinburne and Mellor on the possibility of an afterlife turns on whether there must always be an unambiguous answer to questions about personal identity, even under the strange circumstances envisaged in thought-experiments. Anthony Flew, in relation to these matters, in his *A Disembodied Life?*, reminds us of some of the changes to British philosophy over the last fifty years, and in particular of the influence of Gilbert Ryle's *The Concept of Mind*, published in 1949 – though the changes in general, and Ryle's approach in particular, probably owe something to the then unpublished work of Wittgenstein during the 1930s and 40s. In his book, Ryle mocks and rejects the dualist picture of the mind as being a 'ghost in the machine'; but perhaps his greater achievement, was that, in this and earlier works, he contributed to the change in the prevailing style of philosophical argument. Ryle insisted that philosophical problems arise because we unconsciously make bad inferences from ordinary uses of words to abstract conclusions. These conclusions then puzzle us, but the way to avoid bafflement is to attend more carefully to the original, ordinary use of the words in question. If we are sufficiently sensitive, we will detect the illegitimate move from everyday premises to abstract and maybe paradoxical philosophical conclusions. For a time this approach dominated English philosophy, though the conviction that all philosophical questions arise from muddles about language is now less widespread than it once was. There is an important question of quite what the relationship is or should be between, on the one hand, ordinary language use and beliefs of common sense and, on the other hand, philosophical investigations and theories.

Nigel Warburton's deathbed dialogue takes up an argument made by the mathematician Blaise Pascal (1623-1662). Pascal used a mathematical technique now called 'decision theory' to argue that it is more prudent to believe in God than not; this is because the cost of error to an atheist is an eternity of torment, whereas the cost of error to a theist is negligible. Pascal lived through the later stages of the scientific revolution, and his argument shows some of the characteristics of the modern scientific mind: it is cast in mathematical terms and appeals to prudence to persuade non-believers rather than to properly religious notions such as grace. Nevertheless, it urges belief in a rather old-fashioned and jealous deity, and Pascal's own faith was entirely traditional. Pascal's argument thus reminds us that our thoughts about death are inherited from many different centuries with quite different philosophical and religious tempers, which may not combine easily. Warburton's dialogue runs through some of the argument's flaws: the argument, for example, assumes that there is only one possible god, and that this god is not offended by people who believe in Him out of prudence.

The final part of this collection is a paper written a few years too early for the Humanist Philosophers' Group conference – in fact, over two hundred years too early. It is a letter by the economist Adam Smith, which describes the last days, in 1776, of his friend the atheist philosopher David Hume. Hume's steady good cheer during his final illness was widely remarked on at the time. James Boswell in particular was amazed that Hume could calmly face death without the consolation of religion. It does not seem to have occurred to Boswell that the prospect of Hell-fire might be somewhat less consoling than that of oblivion. Like many intellectuals of the mid-eighteenth century, Hume was deeply read in, and influenced by, the classical civilisations of ancient Greece and Rome. We learn from Smith that Hume entertained himself during his illness by reading Lucian's *Dialogues of the Dead*, in which the dead offer excuses to Charon, the boatman of the Styx. Charon, of course, rejects every excuse and insists that the dead enter his boat to cross to the underworld. It seems that Hume treated death with the same mixture of philosophical seriousness and literary delight that he brought to everything else. There is in this something of the stoic virtue of treating death with the same indifference as every other turn of fate, except that Hume cultivated an amused indifference rather than the grim fortitude usually associated with stoicism.

Evidently Hume wished to die well, that is to say in conformity with the manner of his life. Moreover, his friends seem to have been determined to testify that he did die well. This theme, of the publicly recorded good death, lies at the historical root of Western philosophy in the person of Socrates. As Plato tells it in the *Phaedo*, Socrates chose execution by hemlock rather than escape; he did this out of philosophical conviction and deference to the laws of Athens. Death is also a preoccupation of eighteenth century classicism. This is seen, for example, in the paintings of Jacques-Louis David (1748-1825), which depict the deaths of Socrates, Marat, Lepeletier and Bara, and also include *The Lictors Bring to Brutus the Bodies of His Sons*. In all these paintings death is dignified and morally serious.

If the moment of death is given this importance, then the temptation to falsify it looms. An earlier atheist, La Mettrie, was said to have died of gluttony and to have called on Jesus with his dying breath; yet the most reliable testimony gives no credit to these claims. The story seems to have been put about to defame La Mettrie and discredit his radical materialism. Since Hume was a famous atheist, it is quite likely that his friends were anxious that nothing of the sort should happen to his reputation after his death. Whatever the motives of the friends of Hume, we have in their testimony a model of equanimity in the face to death to match that of Socrates – and, unlike Socrates, Hume did not depend for his peace of mind on the promise of an afterlife.

Intimations of Immortality

John Harris

We are all 'designed' to age and die, but is this simply a design fault? If cells weren't programmed to age, if the telomeres, which govern the number of times a cell may divide, didn't shorten with each division, if our bodies could repair damage due to disease and ageing 'from within', we would certainly live much longer and healthier lives. New research is being reported which would not only constitute major contributions to the treatment of disease, but which could in principle lead to the indefinite extension of life, to the extent perhaps that we would begin to think of people who had received such life-extending treatment as immortals.

Cloned human embryonic stem cells (ES cells), appropriately reprogrammed, might be made to colonise particular tissue and organs triggering constant re-generation. Precise combinations of growth factors injected directly into muscle or tissue might put the body into a state of constant renewal. If we can discover all the genes that trigger the ageing process and switch them off in the early embryo, we could then 'write immortality into the genes of the human race'.[1]

We should note that immortality is not the same as invulnerability, and even these 'immortals' could die or be killed. We do not know when, or even if, such techniques could be developed and made safe enough to use. It might happen in ten, or a thousand years, or never, but many reputable scientists believe it to be possible.

Are we masters of our destiny?

Increased longevity and its logical extension – some would say its *reductio ad absurdum* – immortality have a long history. Certainly the human imagination is familiar with the idea of immortals and mortals living alongside one another, interacting and interbreeding. *The Iliad*, *Odyssey*, *Ramayana* and also the works of Shakespeare have all made such ideas familiar. What imaginative sources have largely ignored are the ethical and political consequences of such possibilities.

---

[1] These possibilities were rehearsed in BBC TV Horizon programme 'Life and Death in the 21st Century' broadcast in January 2000. The quotation is from Lee Silver.

A vital ethical and social question is how should we view the prospect of 'writing immortality into the genes of the human race' or even the prospect of the indefinite extension of individual lives, and whether we can legitimately do anything to stop it?

It is important to press this question for a number of reasons. The first is perhaps its intrinsic interest and importance, for extending lifespan is far from unproblematically beneficial and there are huge questions of justice, of social policy and of sheer practicality to be resolved. Moreover, although the development of this technology may be far in the future there is some considerable importance to addressing the moral and social issues raised by new technologies in advance of their development. There are many good reasons for this. Once a technology has been developed it acquires its own momentum and may be very difficult to stop or control. Equally, fears that are provoked in the panic that can follow dramatic developments may prove unfounded; and acting precipitately on those fears may cut us off from real and substantial benefits. This I believe has been the case with the reaction to the development of cloning technology. 'Horizon scanning' is not simply voyeuristic; it can enable us to choose the futures that we want to experience and to prepare sensibly for those futures. Or, it can forearm us against futures, which, while undesired, are not such as we can legitimately or realistically prevent.

Global justice

One thing we do know is that the technology required to produce considerably longer life-spans will be expensive. For existing people, with multiple interventions probably required, the costs will be substantial. For future generations, people will have to be determinedly circumspect about procreation and will probably need to use reproductive technologies to have their immortal children. Even in technologically advanced countries 'immortality' or increased life expectancy is likely to be confined to a tiny minority of the population. In global terms, the divide between high-income and low-income countries will be increased.

We will face the prospect of parallel populations, of 'mortals' and of 'immortals' existing alongside one another. This, of course, is precisely the destiny for which the poetic imagination has prepared us, literally from 'time immemorial'. While such parallel populations seem inherently undesirable, it is not clear that we could, or even that we should, do anything about preventing such a prospect for reasons of justice or morality. For if immortality or increased life expectancy is a good, it is doubtful ethics to deny palpable goods to some people because we cannot provide them for all. We don't refuse kidney transplants to some patients unless and until we can provide them for all with renal failure. We don't usually regard ourselves as wicked in Europe because we perform many such transplants while low-income countries perform few or none at all.

And this unfairness is not simply contingent, the function of a regrettable, but in principle removable, lack of resources. There will always be circumstances in which we cannot prevent harms nor do good to everyone; but no one, I hope, thinks that this affords us a reason to decline to prevent harms to anyone. If twins suffer from cancer and one is incurable and the other not, we do not conclude that we should not treat the curable cancer because this would be unjust to the incurable twin.

Is longevity a good?

This brings us to the central issue: would substantially increased life expectancy or even immortality be a benefit, a good? There are people who regard the prospect of immortality with distaste or even horror; there are others who desire it above all else. In that most people fear death and want to postpone it as long as possible, there is some reason to suppose that the prospect of personal immortality would be widely welcomed. But it is one thing to contemplate our own immortality, quite another to contemplate a world in which increasing numbers of people were immortal, and in which all or any future children would have to compete indefinitely with previous generations for jobs, space and everything else.

Even if such a prospect made immortality seem unattractive, it is not clear what ethically could be done to prevent the development and utilisation of techniques for substantially increasing longevity and even engineering immortality. Remember that immortality is not unconnected with preventing or curing a whole range of serious diseases. It is one thing to ask the question, 'Should we make people immortal?' and answer in the negative; quite another to ask whether we should make people immune to heart disease, cancer, dementia and many other diseases and decide that we shouldn't.

It might be appropriate to think of immortality as the, possibly unwanted, side effect of treating or preventing a whole range of diseases. Could we really say to people, 'You must die at the age of thirty or forty or fifty, because the only way we can cure you is to make you immortal or let you live to be two or three hundred?' Faced with such a choice an individual might well say, 'Let me have my three score and ten and then let me die'.

Uncharted waters

How are we to think about the ethics of increasing longevity and even achieving immortality for some people and perhaps even, eventually, for very many people?

Is there a moral difference between a future that will contain x billion people succeeded by another x billion different people and so on indefinitely, or a future in which x billion people living indefinitely and replacing themselves on the (rare?) occasions when they are killed? In short, we are asking whether what matters morally is that life years of reasonable quality exist or that different people with lives of reasonable quality exist. Put in this way the problem assumes a familiar form – should we maximise life years or individuals' lives?

Whatever we feel about the answer to this question, there are other reasons why we should be in favour of the creation of new human individuals. One group of such reasons has to do with the desire to procreate and the pleasures of having and rearing children. These I will not discuss further now, although, in that they are fairly universal desires and pleasures, they have some importance.

The second and more germane set of reasons has to do with the advantages of fresh people, fresh ideas and the possibility of continued evolution or at least development. If these reasons are powerful, we might be facing a future in which the fairest and the most ethical course is to go in for a sort of 'generational cleansing'. This would involve deciding collectively how long it is reasonable for people to live in each generation and trying to ensure that as many as possible live healthy lives of that length. We would then have to ensure that, having lived a 'fair innings', they died (suicide or euthanasia?) in order to make way for future generations.

While this might seem desirable, it is difficult to imagine how enforcing it could be justified, at least if our time honoured ethical principles remain unreformed. For how could a society resolve to deliberately curtail worthwhile life, while maintaining a commitment to the sanctity of life?

If we cannot face modifying our conception of the sanctity of life, there are other strategies open. For example, we might, if we could, do something that amounts to the same thing, namely programme cells to switch off the ageing-process for a certain time, and then switch it back on again when a 'fair innings' had been reached. This of course would be much like the system nature has in place, with the important difference that most people would live a full life span rather than having to run the gauntlet of the genetic lottery or the risks of infection.

The fair innings solution to the problem of immortality requires not simply that people's lives are not further sustained once a fair innings has been achieved, but rather we are asked to contemplate ensuring the deaths of those who have passed their sell-by date. If this is not done, only a few of the immortals will die when they should, only those, in short, who require life-sustaining measures in order to go on living.

But the contemplation of making sure that people who wish to go on living cannot do so, is terrible indeed.

Immortality and reproduction

Faced with the problem of formulating an appropriate population policy for immortals, and of dealing with some of the inequities their existence creates, society might be tempted to offer people immortality-producing therapies, but only on condition that they did not reproduce, except perhaps posthumously. People would be permitted to become immortal, but perhaps only to have children by assisted reproductive techniques after their own deaths, or on condition that they switch off their immortality (assuming that to be possible) in order to have children. Initially this strategy will be marginal because many people will need therapies only after they have reproduced, but as the techniques become routine people will want to secure their immortality earlier. An alternative strategy would involve would-be immortals agreeing, on reproducing, to forfeit their subsequent right to life-prolonging therapies. These possibilities raise important ethical issues. A major problem is that reproductive liberty is a powerful and widely accepted right protected by the major international conventions on human rights. It would be difficult to justify curtailing this right and even more difficult to police any proposed curtailment. There are also major issues about whether or not it would be good for children if mortals produced immortal children or if immortal parents produced mortal children.

Certainly we should be slow to reject cures for terrible diseases even if the 'price' we have to pay for those cures is increasing life expectancy or even immortality in recipients. It is unlikely that we can stop progression to increased life spans and even immortality, and it is doubtful whether we could produce coherent ethical objections. Better surely to start thinking now about how we can live decently and creatively both with the prospect and with the reality of such lives.

Six Months to Live

Tim LeBon

> '*Time is very precious for me at the moment, as I have been told I have only six months to live. I'm an atheist, so can't go to a priest to help me face up to death. However I do feel the urgent need to take stock of my life and really try to make the most of what is left. Would philosophical counselling be worth my time?'*

Alex

Philosophical counselling is a form of practical philosophy, the aim of which is to help individuals reflect wisely on their lives and cope with 'problems in living' such as relationship problems, career dilemmas – and 'end of life' issues such as Alex's. In this article, after a brief overview of philosophical counselling, I hope to show how it could be of help to Alex and others like her.

Although its routes can be traced back to Socrates, modern philosophical counselling began in 1981, when Gerd Achenbach opened his first philosophical practice in Germany. Philosophical counselling has since spread over the world, notably to the United States where much publicity has surrounded Lou Marinoff and his book *Plato Not Prozac!* In Britain the rise of philosophical counselling owes much to the Society for Philosophy in Practice (SPP). SPP organised the *Fifth International Conference on Philosophy in Practice* in Oxford in 1999 and it keeps a register of practising philosophical counsellors.

Philosophical counselling is perhaps best seen as a hybrid of applied philosophy and conventional Rogerian counselling. A philosophical counsellor will help you engage in a mutual philosophical enquiry rather than just reflect what you have said back empathically in the hope that it leads to your personal growth. Philosophical counsellors use similar philosophical methods to those of academic philosophers, except that, rather than apply them on their own to an abstract problem, they apply them in collaboration with the client to a concrete issue in the client's life.

So how might philosophical counselling proceed for Alex?

The exact course of philosophical counselling would depend very much on what Alex wanted; for some, having a space to reflect for themselves is the most important aspect, whereas others might specifically want to have their perspective challenged philosophically. Alex's initial statement implies that, like most people, she wants a mixture of support and challenge; with matters of life and death, particular sensitivity is obviously called for. With these caveats in mind, what follows is a sketch of one route that philosophical counselling with Alex might take.

Alex talks about facing up to death, so a good place to start would be an enquiry into the nature of death. Being an atheist, Alex would probably dismiss the notion of an afterlife out of hand, but it would be worth briefly checking the grounds for this dismissal. Is it the strong claim that the idea of living after one's body has ceased to function is incoherent, or the more modest assertion that we have no good reason to believe in an afterlife? Shakespeare (through Hamlet) suggested that death is 'the undiscovered country from whose bourn no traveller returns', but philosophical reflection might cast doubt on speaking about death as a country, even metaphorically. In contrast, Epicurus maintained that 'when death is there, we are not, and when we are there, death is not'. The question which Alex would be asked to consider is whether death is a state of oneself (like being unconscious) or whether it is a non-state (like before we were conceived). The distinction is important, because, as Hamlet recognised, the thought of being in a completely different state is indeed frightening – whereas Epicurus argued that since death isn't something we experience, there is no good reason to be anxious about it. Epicurus's argument is reinforced by Lucretius's comparison between the time after we die with the time before we were born; we don't consider the aeons before we were born a disaster, so why should we think differently about the period following our death? Alex might be referred to Nagel's excellent *Mortal Questions* or *What Does it All Mean?* if she wanted to pursue these questions further.

Such discussion may well convince Alex that an atheist has a lot less to fear from death than a Christian, who may indeed have grounds for anguish about the possibility of hell-fire. But she may say that we haven't yet addressed her main concern, which is more to do with the absence of the positive benefits of living than the negative aspects of death itself. Some philosophers (notably Bernard Williams) have argued that immortality would not really be such a good thing; it would be very boring. It's hard to imagine Alex being persuaded by this argument, but perhaps a Kantian thought-experiment along the lines of 'What would it be like if everyone lived forever?' might give pause for thought. Clearly if we did all go on living, there would be insufficient resources for future generations; what's more, if previous generations had been bestowed the gift of immortality, it is highly unlikely that we would have lived at all. Perhaps dying is our ultimate, albeit involuntary, gift to future generations. Richard Dawkins has argued that in a sense we are immortal – through the transmission of our genes and memes. If Alex has children, her genes will survive; in any case her memes – replicas of her ideas – will continue their existence. If she has written a poem, contributed to a movement, or just passed on her ideas to her friends and family, then, to the extent that she *is* these thoughts, she will carry on living. Alex might well counter this by saying that it blurs the distinction between her memes and her*self*; she might well sympathise with Woody Allen who said 'I don't want to achieve immortality through my work – I want to achieve it through not dying'.

If this was her reaction, we could usefully move from talking about death to talking about life. Alex said she wants to make the most of the time she has left, so how can she do this? A philosophical counsellor is particularly well equipped to help someone think through what really matters to them. A starting point might be a consideration of what atheistic philosophers have thought. Did she agree with Richard Robinson's list of values in his classic work *An Atheist's Values* – beauty, truth, reason, love and conscientiousness? What in *her* life had she found to be of most value? In my book *Wise Therapy* I describe a procedure – RSVP – which aims to help people work out what values are really most important to them. Such a process would serve two purposes for Alex – to allow her to take stock of her life and also to think about how to use her remaining time as best she could. We might even discuss the concept of a 'good death' – what would she have to do between now and the time she died in order to feel that she had done as much she could?

Existential therapist Irvin Yalom has noticed, in his work with terminally ill cancer patients, that there is often a rearrangement of life's priorities, an enhanced sense of living in the present, a deeper communication with loved ones and more willingness to take risks. Alex's interest in philosophical counselling might well reflect the fact that this 'trivialising of the trivial' has already begun. Philosophical counselling cannot give Alex more time, which is what she would really like, but it might just help her to fully see the value and meaning that is already latent in her life – and to make the most of her remaining days.

Voluntary Sex

Peter Cave

> *'Were voluntary euthanasia permitted, we should slide down a slippery slope; we should end up permitting involuntary euthanasia. Many of the elderly would find themselves pressurized into dying prematurely – in one way or another – and against their will. Perhaps society would make them feel that they had become too burdensome. Perhaps relatives would see an easy way to get their hands on the inheritances – in order to pay for the next exotic holiday, or to live a lifestyle they had always envied, or simply to pay off the mortgage. The acceptance of voluntary euthanasia would send us skidding down into this murky miserable mire for the aged and ill – one which paradoxically would be more threatening to the well-heeled, weak and elderly than those on their uppers.'*

If, as the above argument contends, slippery slopes can be so very very slippery, we should find people worried about sliding down these slopes in other areas of life. Do we? Well, luckily we have come across such people – people who, because of their slippery, sliding and skidding worries, practise a distinctive way of living. They are members of the Order of the Non-Copulatory; they offer irrefutable reasoning that establishes sexual intercourse to be morally wrong. Members of the Order – shunners of slippery slopes, indeterminacy and greyness to a man and to a woman – advance a black and white case; but do they make out a good case or is there something radically wrong in their reasoning? If there is something wrong, does it show the slippery slope argument against voluntary euthanasia also to be wrong – or is there some morally relevant difference?

Novice: Formerly I delighted in fornication, but now I realize the folly of my viceful ways. Remind me, Sister, of the reasons why sexual intercourse – voluntary sexual intercourse, for I did nothing against anyone's wishes – is so evil.

Sister Cecilia: It is as clear as the proposition that two plus two equals four, though arguably and happily it does not possess the same degree of clarity as that of the truth of Fermat's last theorem and Sister Ethel's potato and elderberry home-made wine. The reasoning may be summed up in the words 'slippery slope'. Voluntary intercourse must not be permitted for otherwise society would slip into the ruination of enforced fornication, of involuntary intercourse.

Novice: Ah, yes, I remember. You are following the teachings of many – particularly precious papery pundits who deal with related ethical issues of similar gravity, for example, those of euthanasia. They show how wrong euthanasia is. They are of the Order of To Order To Keep Going Come What May, are they not?

Sister Cecilia: Indeed, you are right, though their order to keep going does not, of course, apply to the sexual act. But, yes, 'Keep Going' fairly sums up their position, just as 'Stop Coming' is an abbreviation for ours.

Novice: Please remind me how the teachings lead us to the truth on this matter.

Sister Cecilia: Nothing could be simpler. One basic problem is that voluntary sex (to use the colloquial abbreviation) may not be truly voluntary just as, indeed, voluntary euthanasia may not be truly voluntary.

Novice: So, we might sometimes get the two confused. Therefore voluntary sex is wrong even when we have not confused it with the involuntary..?

Sister Cecilia: Quite so and...

Sister Severe: This deep difficulty of not knowing what is truly so, indeed an epistemic difficulty, pervades our lives. As you know, you cannot be sure that low fat spread is not butter, yet nor that it is butter, yet nor that you can't believe it's not butter. Well, that's why you won't find me eating anything like that – and as for those other things you're not sure about – meat-filled sausages, French cheeses from Somerset and holidays of a life-time...

Sister Cecilia: Now, now, that is sufficient buttering and butting in, Sister Severe. You don't want to become like Sister Silly who, because she once mistook her brother for a hat, thinks it's best to treat all hats as her brothers and all the Brothers as her hats.

Novice: Ah, so this is just a general epistemic problem about when and whether we know certain things, but on some occasions do we not know when sexual consent is, indeed, consent? And on those occasions...

Sister Cecilia: Never mind all that. Those opposed to voluntary euthanasia have another knock-down consideration, namely, that voluntary euthanasia leads inexorably to involuntary euthanasia. Now, this consideration applies all the more to sexual engagements in life's carnal carnival.

Novice: Ah, I understand. In lands where sexual intercourse on a voluntary basis is permitted, you can witness inexorable sexual leadings, taking us from 'yes' meaning 'yes' to 'yes' meaning 'yes, but' and then meaning 'eh, well, all right then' which might be meaning 'must you?' – and then a dozy sigh means sometimes 'maybe, yes' and sometimes 'maybe, no' and sometimes 'go away – oh, if you must!'; and yet each change is so small that if sexual intercourse is permitted in the one case, it should be equally permitted in the other. Perils of plied alcohol, persuasive words ('oh, just this once'), of job offers, casting couches and dinner dates – of 'it's all for the sake of the film' – lead us through a whole range of date rapes and acquaintance rapes and 'for the sake of art' rapes; and these could all be morally justified courtesy of the slope, that wicked, wicked slippery slope.

Sister Cecilia: Quite – and it is the very possibility of all of these fine gradations that shows there is no real difference between the voluntary and the involuntary.

Novice: Now you mention it, it is indeed truly astonishing that society believes it can draw the voluntary/involuntary sexual distinction when it is so fuzzy.

Sister Cecilia: Perfectly correct. Our Order firmly believes that if it is at all possible for A not to be clearly discerned from B, then if B is discredited, so too must be A. Rape is discredited and so therefore must be all sexual intercourse, voluntary versions included.

Sister Severe: And more! When I look at the colour spectrum, greens merge into blues. I see night merging into day, wakefulness into sleepingness, beginnings into ends and the M1 into the M6. So much the worse, I declare, for colours, for day, for...

Novice: But musing upon all of this a little – if you're right, then you've just turned the slope round and are sliding in the other direction, from rape being wrong to voluntary intercourse being wrong; but if one slide ought not to be made, then maybe the other also ought not to be. After all, people may voluntarily browse in bookshops, whistle a tune or check the time, yet we don't fear sliding down slopes whereby, in the end, people will be frogmarched to the bookshops, forced to whistle or threatened with gaol if not checking the clock.

Sister Cecilia: Now, now, that's enough, all of you – especially you, Sister Severe! A new member of our Order must be taught how not to run before she's taught how not to walk, let alone how not to...

Sister Severe: My very point again – for running cannot be clearly distinguished from walking and nor walking from dawdling – and dawdling can amount to hanging around and no foot movement at all.

Novice: But do not people talk of their right to engage in voluntary sex? Do they not also speak of personal autonomy here?

Sister Cecilia: True, but personal autonomy is not the most important factor at all. After all, no one should complain that they are prevented from acting in ways which would harm others.

Novice: Yet if a couple engages in voluntary sex, they are probably harming no one at all.

Similarly, if someone is helped to die in their interests and according to their wants, then, well, that is voluntary euthanasia and it seems it is compassionate and…

Sister Cecilia: Ah, you are forgetting about the further slippery effects – those on society. If voluntary euthanasia becomes acceptable, then we are making judgements about life's value and we may cause others to reflect on their own lives and think they should put an end to living too. So too, if people engage in voluntary sex, they are making a judgement about the quality of life, about what is valuable in life, and so they may affect others, causing the frail and vulnerable – and virgins! – to give way to their passions or even causing them to think they possess lusts when, truly, they are lustless and listless. But for the rampant sexual ethos, these weak individuals would be without list and without lust.

Novice: Ah, yes, I forgot that in such actions, I am also responsible for what others do in society at large through my effects on society. I must remember that. Even if someone is strongly opposed to involuntary intercourse and herself engages only in the voluntary, none the less, indeed by that very engagement, she bears some responsibility for the violent rapists and persuasion rapists and date rapists and 'have another drink' rapists and 'wouldn't you like promotion' rapists and so on. But tell me, how do we expect our Order ultimately to have any members at all, if all sex is wrong?

Sister Cecilia: Oh, dear me, you are about to confuse having sex with procreating. Those opposed to euthanasia clearly explain how people sometimes confuse killing with seeking to relieve a patient's distress by a means which you know will happen to hasten death. Killing involves an intention to bring about death; relieving patients' distress involves no such intention. So, we may intend to procreate and even know that it will involve using those funny bits of our bodies in funny ways, but the intercourse of those funny bodily bits is not something that we intend to have.

Novice: Ah yes, I had forgotten about the subtlety of the distinction between what we intend to do and what we happen to know or foresee will be the outcome – in what, I believe, is known as the Doctrine of Double Effect – though I had not encountered its being used in quite the curious way round that you suggest. But anyway, in such cases is there really a morally relevant distinction between foreseeing and intending? And can we ever be sure that someone truly is only foreseeing and not intending? After all you raised such a worry earlier on with the voluntary/involuntary distinction? Is there not a slippery slope here?

Sister Cecilia: Now, now, I hope that you are not going to become a logic chopper like all those so-called philosophers and conceptual analysts and those oh so sensible rational humanist types and...

Novice: Indeed not, I acknowledge your wisdom. Tell me, though, why is that member – the one over there – so very, very quiet?

Sister Cecilia: You've spotted Sister Silent. She has true enlightenment, fully grasping the greyness of the world. She sees how all good things can slide into bad, how all truth can lead to falsity, how the whole world is one big slope, yet even how slope-ness itself is sloppy and slippery, sliding from the horizontal to the vertical. As a result, she thinks nothing and says nothing and does nothing.

All: She must be truly blessed.

Is There a Right to Die?

Suzanne Uniacke

Do we have a right to die? At least one writer has remarked that it seems odd to speak of our having a right to something that will inevitably happen to us all. As with many other purported rights, whether we can plausibly be said to have a right to die depends to a considerable extent on what this right is supposed to include and what it is taken to imply.

This short essay examines only one particular aspect of the right to die, namely the legal right, which is the legal permissibility, of suicide and what this might be taken to imply about the legalisation of voluntary euthanasia. The question I shall address is whether, as some people maintain, the legalisation of voluntary euthanasia can be defended as an extension of the fact that suicide is not illegal. In my view the answer to this question is 'no'. To avert possible misunderstanding, it is important to stress here that to reject the idea that voluntary euthanasia should be legalised as an extension of the legality of suicide is not to imply that the legalisation of voluntary euthanasia cannot be defended on other grounds. On the contrary, because attempts to argue for the legalisation of voluntary euthanasia from the legal permissibility of suicide are conceptually and morally distorted, they detract from a more plausible case for the legalisation of voluntary euthanasia. Such attempts represent a wider trend amongst some philosophers who seek to justify voluntary euthanasia from the fact that it is *voluntary*, that is, on the basis that the subject himself consents to being killed. This line of argument loses sight of the appropriate role of the subject's consent in medical treatment (including proposed euthanasia). In so doing, it can lead to instances of killing being described and defended as voluntary 'euthanasia' that are no such thing. This line of argument also diverts attention away from a more appropriate argument for the legalisation of genuine voluntary euthanasia.

The right of suicide

Is there a right of suicide – a right to kill oneself? And if there is, could a right to kill oneself imply a right to be killed by another person at one's own request? In answering these questions I begin with the thought that if, as competent adults, we have a right to suicide *simpliciter* – that is, a right that exists absolutely, without limitation, reservation or just in certain respects – then this can only be a right of non-interference: a right not to be prevented by coercive means from intentionally bringing about our own deaths. An unqualified right of suicide such as this would be grounded in what is called 'negative freedom': such a right would be an aspect of the right of a competent adult to act without coercive interference in ways that she believes are in her interests, or which she believes will preserve, enhance or extend her freedom, even if in fact what she does will undermine, restrict or thwart these things.

The legal right of suicide is such an unqualified, general right: it is a right that does not derive from or depend upon the circumstances or the reasons why the person wants to commit suicide. More specifically, the legal right of suicide has two central features. It is a permission, a right of non-interference; and on that basis (as a right of non-interference) it is accorded to competent adults irrespective of their reasons for wanting to kill themselves. We are legally free to commit suicide even in circumstances where suicide is morally indefensible; this might be because, for example, it is an act of revenge that is intended to destroy the happiness of another person; or it is a cowardly shirking of responsibility; or it involves defaulting on one's obligations to dependants.

Should this legal right of suicide extend to a general right of voluntary assistance from other people where a competent person *for whatever reason* wants to kill herself but can't do so or can't do so without great unpleasantness? Surely the answer is no. Think of a case in which a young healthy person wants, for whatever reason, to commit suicide but can't or can't without great unpleasantness. She requests your assistance and you are in a position to kill her – perhaps you are the only one in a position to do so. Would you unreasonably restrict or infringe her freedom in declining to assist her in this way? Say you do voluntarily assist her: you kill her, and you do so simply on the grounds that it is not illegal for her to kill herself irrespective of her reason for so doing. In this case, is your killing her clearly something that is not the law's business or that should have no legal (criminal) implications? It seems to me, again, that the answer to these questions is 'no'.

I emphasise this last point in order to highlight the fact that arguments that support the legalisation of voluntary euthanasia as an extension of the legality of suicide are not urging legalisation of voluntary euthanasia as such – they are not defending voluntary euthanasia as *euthanasia*. Rather, in maintaining that euthanasia is simply a matter of allowing people who want to die to get assistance from others who are willing to help them, such arguments characterise voluntary euthanasia as an aspect of a purported *general* freedom or right of assisted suicide *for whatever reason*. But in cases of euthanasia we are *not* talking about assisting people who want to die for whatever reason. Euthanasia is colloquially called 'mercy killing' and in such cases the motive for wanting to assist someone who wants to die is not simply her wish to end her life, irrespective of the reason. Rather, it is the fact that due to terminal illness or unbearable suffering the person's life has in fact become intolerable. What grounds the moral case for euthanasia is appropriate compassion for a person in these circumstances. This is consistent with the way in which euthanasia is typically characterised and defended.

What euthanasia is

The term 'euthanasia' usually refers to intentionally bringing about a merciful death for a dying person to spare them pointless suffering. 'Euthanasia' is now also used to refer to bringing about the death of someone whose life is judged not worth going on with because, for example, she is irretrievably comatose or in a persistent vegetative state. There is now a standard distinction drawn between voluntary, non-voluntary, and involuntary euthanasia. This distinction refers to the matter of the *consent of the subject* of euthanasia. Voluntary euthanasia is with the consent of the subject; non-voluntary euthanasia refers to cases in which the subject is incapable of giving or withholding consent (for example, because comatose or an infant). Euthanasia is involuntary when performed without the consent of a competent subject. Whether it is performed with the subject's consent or otherwise, euthanasia is a form of homicide of another person on compassionate grounds. Compassion for someone who is terminally ill or in unbearable pain is of course insufficient to justify euthanasia, even according to those who believe that euthanasia can be justified in these circumstances. One reason is the respect that is due to the wishes of the subject, the person who might be mercifully killed. A person's wish not to be killed is a moral constraint against performing an act of euthanasia. It would be morally impermissible mercifully to kill a dying person who does not want to go on living (she might hope she dies soon), but who does not want to be killed. In cases of voluntary euthanasia, the consent of the subject is held to remove this particular constraint.

Of course the relationship between the quality of a person's life, according to a set of objective criteria (such as that the subject is terminally ill or in unbearable pain), and the person's own priorities and perception of the value of her life can be a very difficult matter. At one extreme, a dying person might value every minute of a life that is wracked with intense, unrelenting pain, and for which death would reasonably be seen as a merciful release; at the other extreme, another person might see little or no value in her life when, from a more objective perspective, it contains much that is of positive value. The condition under which a person's life has become intolerable, so as not to be worth going on with, is not a completely objective matter, to be determined by a set of criteria independently of the subject's own priorities and perception of the value of her own life. But neither is it a completely subjective matter, wholly dependent on whether or not the subject herself regards her life as worth living. To kill someone does not qualify as an act of euthanasia (mercy killing) simply in virtue of the fact that the subject no longer values her life and wants to die. Legalisation of voluntary euthanasia would require very careful specification of the conditions affecting the subject who wishes to be killed; the criteria under which the law might permit acts of voluntary euthanasia would need to include conditions that are appropriate to ensuring that what is permitted is genuinely euthanasia.

Philosophical slippery slopes

Many philosophers who argue for the legalisation of voluntary euthanasia dismiss so-called slippery slope arguments that maintain that if we permit voluntary euthanasia this would lead to *involuntary* euthanasia or to killings that, although voluntary, are *not euthanasia* (for example, where people might be killed who are not terminally ill or in great pain, but who for some other reason want to die). However, the philosophical debate about euthanasia has itself given rise to some disturbing slippery slopes, for example, where instances of killing that are not euthanasia are defended under the guise of euthanasia. I have in mind here a prominent utilitarian defence of so-called 'euthanasia' of infants with Down Syndrome or haemophilia.

The argument for the legalisation of voluntary euthanasia from the legal permissibility of suicide also involves a worrying slide. If it is maintained that a competent person's own decision that she wants to die is itself a sufficient reason for the legality of assistance when she cannot kill herself, then this looks very much like the bottom of a slope that opponents of the legalisation of voluntary euthanasia are concerned about. In fact people who oppose the legalisation of voluntary euthanasia might be less concerned at the prospect of its leading to cases of involuntary and non-voluntary killing that are genuinely *euthanasia*, than about the implications of a legal right to be killed at one's own request that is derived from an appeal to the legal freedom that we all have to commit suicide.

The right to die

Suicide is not illegal. Further, we are legally entitled to refuse life-saving or life-prolonging medical treatment. Both of these legal permissions are rights that competent persons have against coercive interference, irrespective of their reasons for wanting to end their lives. In contrast, a legal right of voluntary euthanasia would be a right of positive assistance to die; more precisely, it would be a legal permission to be killed by another person, with one's consent, because one's life has become intolerable due to terminal illness or unbearable suffering. The case for voluntary euthanasia as a legal permission of assistance to die must be based on the two conditions just mentioned: it must be grounded in the fact that what is proposed is euthanasia; and the subject's consent to being killed should then be seen as removing a constraint that would otherwise overrule compassionate killing. As the law stands, the consent of the subject of homicide is not a general defence to murder, and it is right that this be so.

It is one thing to hold that the fact that a competent adult wants to die, for whatever reason, justifies the legal permissibility of suicide as a right of non-interference. It is quite another thing to hold that a person's wish to die, for whatever reason, can justify the legalisation of assistance from others.

How Should We Treat the Dead?

Piers Benn

Most societies have deeply held views about correct behaviour with respect to the dead. For example, there are rules and rituals connected with the disposal of corpses. Great importance is attached to treating the dead with respect: it is thought bad form to speak ill of the (recently) dead, and wrong to ignore the instructions in wills. Such things are regarded as important even by many people who do not believe there is any personal survival of death. But this raises a conundrum. Can the dead literally benefit or be harmed by any actions that are performed after their death, if there is no life after death? Why on earth should it matter how we treat the dead, if the dead do not exist as possible subjects of good or ill fortune?

This problem is associated with another one which is more fundamental, and which I propose to tackle first. It goes back at least to Epicurus, who in his *Letter to Menoeceus* tries to debunk popular pagan superstitions about death. He maintains that death is nothing to fear, since he believes – as a philosophical, as opposed to an Ibiza, hedonist – that the only intrinsically good or bad things for us are pleasant and unpleasant experiences, respectively. Since the dead have no experiences, it follows that nothing intrinsically bad can happen to the dead. Admittedly, death is not much to look forward to either, since there will be no pleasant experiences after death. But at least we can be reassured that death is not bad for us; that stories of Hades and punishment after death are false, put about to frighten the credulous.

However, as many writers have pointed out, the main problem with this argument is its assumption of philosophical hedonism. Many pleasant experiences, like our feelings when we hear good news, depend upon our belief that something good has happened. And isn't it the good thing, rather than the experience it generates, that we really value? If I feel happy because I've solved an important problem, then what I really value is my having solved the problem, not the mere fact that I have been made happy. Most people don't want to live in a fool's paradise, in which they bask in pleasure arising from entirely deluded beliefs.

The same goes for misfortunes. Some events are misfortunes, even if we never get to discover about them. If my so-called friends laugh at me behind my back or secretly break promises they have made to me, then I am a victim of wrongdoing and misfortune even though I don't consciously suffer. The point of all this is that, in much of our lives, our happiness and unhappiness depends on our getting, or losing, things we value. But we don't value them merely because they make us happy; we are made happy by them because we value them.

If this is right, it bears both on the evil of death itself, and the evil of other things that happen to us after death, such as having slanderous gossip spread. Perhaps I can reasonably hope for my will to be respected after my death, even if I believe that when the time comes I shall be unaware of whether my will is respected or not.

This argument is fine as far as it goes, but unfortunately there is more to the problem. For Epicurus, almost as an afterthought, comes up with another, quite distinct argument for not fearing death, which could also apply to other supposed misfortunes that befall us after death. This new argument is more worrying. 'Death…is nothing to us, since so long as we exist, death is not with us; but when death comes, then we do not exist.' This is the 'no-subject' problem, and is not concerned with the lack of experience after death. It is about the lack of *existence* after death, and its apparent implications for the evil of death. If the dead do not now exist, then how can anything now be true of them? In particular, how can they now be victims of misfortune? Whether the misfortune consists in some way they are treated (such as having their corpses fed to pigs), or in simply being dead, it is hard to see how they can be victims of good or ill fortune when dead.

Some writers, such as Thomas Nagel, tend to see the evil of death as negative rather than positive. That is, it is essentially the evil of being deprived of good things (life and all its goods) rather than an evil in its own right. But this manoeuvre won't extricate us from Epicurus's challenge. For while we can speak of the evil of deprivation *during life* – for example, the evil of being imprisoned and deprived of normal enjoyments – it does not follow that we can speak of being deprived *of life* as an evil. For if you don't exist, how can you be the victim of even a negative evil, let alone a positive one?

Of course, all this seems absurd; if I could now choose to die or to continue living, I would choose to live – unless my life were so terrible that I would prefer that it ended. And indeed, what is interesting about Epicurus's arguments (and those of his followers, for example, Lucretius) is that while they have an air of sophistry, no one can quite agree on where the errors lie. The thrust of the Epicurean case is that I seemingly cannot say the following thing: that *I* would be better off alive than *I* would be if dead. The reason is that if I am dead, then there is no I.

Perhaps the most ingenious solution to this has come from Fred Feldman in *Confrontations with the Reaper*. This is that the evil of death is not something that strikes at the moment of death, and persists evermore afterwards. It is that death strikes eternally – that is, timelessly – and consists in the finitude of life, of the fact that life does not go on longer than it does. It is not the case that after my death, I am worse off than I would have been if I had not died then. Rather, the tragedy of death is that my lifespan, timelessly conceived, is not longer. No doubt life could be too long – it might become intolerable if it went on for more than a few centuries, as Janacek's opera *The Makropulos Case* suggests (discussed by Bernard Williams, see his *Problems of the Self*). But as things are, many of us could do with a lot more life than we actually get.

But if death can be an evil, can things that occur after my death be evils for me, such as slanderous gossip or being fed to swine? In short, are there better and worse ways of treating me after my death? This is a trickier problem, oddly enough. For these things occur when the putative subject of these ills no longer exists.

This question can arise, in particular, when we consider appropriate and inappropriate ways to treat human corpses. Attitudes to the treatment of dead bodies have varied between cultures and epochs. At one time, dissections and autopsies were thought wrong because they violated the sanctity of the body. Judaism and Islam have strict rules about burial; in particular, it must be carried out very shortly after death. When the bodies of Saddam Hussein's slain sons were shown on television, touched up by morticians so as to persuade the world that the bullet-ridden corpses really were those of Uday and Qusay, there was outrage in the Muslim world. Altering the appearance of the bodies was thought wrong, as was delaying their burial – however brutal the men had been during their short, criminal lives. In the ancient world, there was a disagreement, reported by Herodotus, between the Greeks and the Indian tribe of Callatians concerning cremation and cannibalism. The Greeks abhorred cannibalism, while the Callatians took a dim view of cremation. In our own time, the Roman Catholic Church has only recently come to accept cremation, albeit with great misgivings.

Some of these attitudes and laws are to do with purity, especially in the Jewish religion. But they also derive from a sense of what is owed to the person who 'owned' the body, or, if you like, owed to the body that was the person. Some ways of treating dead bodies show disrespect to the dead. To cut someone's head off (when already dead, that is) and use it as a football would seem, to many, not to be harmless fun with an inanimate object, but an act of desecration. What sort of person would find this amusing? What character does he show? Yet others, no doubt a minority, are prepared to bite the bullet and argue that such acts are not wrong, or at least do no harm to the dead, since the dead cannot be harmed at all. The debate was recently brought to the fore by the Bodyworks exhibition in Brick Lane, London, produced by the German Professor of Anatomy, Gunther von Hagens – he who also performed an 'autopsy' (in fact a dissection) on Channel Four, wearing his trademark hat. I have to admit that I enjoyed the exhibition, which displayed many plastinated bodies and body parts, often arranged in strange and almost comic postures. I was involved in a panel discussion with Professor von Hagens at the Edinburgh Fringe in 2003. One of his main arguments was that he was an educator who was bringing anatomy and dissection to the people, away from the medical elites. He was an enthusiast, a crusader. Certainly he saw nothing degrading or desecrating about the exhibition, though he faced attack from a Professor of Pathology who declared that it told us nothing about either life or death.

I inclined to agree with von Hagens that the exhibition was legitimate *per se*, though I later had doubts about whether the people whose bodies were used had given adequately informed consent. But the philosophical question is about the principle of respect for the dead – is it possible to do wrong in our treatment of bodies, whether or not this or that example of such wrongdoing is a good one? The answer, I suggest, is 'yes'. A corpse is an image of a person who lived, and it is hard to separate our attitudes to living and dead bodies. Yet this doesn't quite answer the original Epicurean challenge: assuming the dead do not exist (although in another sense, there are dead people, in the sense that they can be referred to), can it really be possible to *harm* the dead?

I know of no knock-down answer to this, but simply suggest the following. Just as the evil of death is a timeless evil, so our interests can exist timelessly, and their satisfaction or frustration need not be coincident with the life of the bearer of those interests. An author with a desire for a literary reputation might reasonably hope to be remembered after his or her death. More obviously, most of us wish to be remembered lovingly by those we loved – indeed, a world in which the dead were not mourned by their relatives and friends would be a much worse world, even if containing less painful grief, than one where the dead were missed and grieved over. And, quite apart from our musings about the metaphysical conundrums, we should keep the lived human world at the centre of our focus, and the attitudes that no virtuous person lacks: a sense of the dead as still having interests, and a sense of their continued membership of a moral community. While studying the Epicurean challenge is challenging, we should keep in place the values and emotions surrounding death and its inevitability.

Dead People

Peter Cave

We should treat people well;
therefore, we should treat dead people well.

Many would brush aside this minimal argument – hereafter, *The Extensive Embrace* – and the brushing would be big with contempt; but, after some explanation, the argument should be seen as good and the conclusion accepted. To resist the conclusion is – let us quip (recalling the quick, that is, the living, as opposed to the dead) – *quickist*; it manifests a prejudice in favour of the quickly quick over the slowed-down quick, namely, the dead.

Here are some objections – a baker's dozen – from the living. Allow me to reply on behalf of the dead.

Objection 1: Dead people are not people (I).

The term 'dead people' is self-contradictory, if taken to imply that any such items really are people. Incomplete circles are no circles, forged banknotes no banknotes and dead persons no persons. If an item is a red square, then the item is red and a square; but counterfeit coins of the realm are no coins of the realm. The incomplete, forged and counterfeit features undermine the status of the circles, banknotes and coins respectively; the feature of being dead undermines the items being persons (if items there be). All we have are the corpses – if that. So, how we should treat people has no direct bearing on the dead, the dead being no people at all.

Reply to Objection 1

Certainly, The Extensive Embrace is not directly concerned with corpses; certainly, the argument rests on no assumption that dead people are somehow shadowy, incomplete – or better, over-done – people still in existence. The argument concerns those individuals who once lived and no longer do – those individuals who once were people and no longer are. There is nothing contradictory in speaking of such individuals, just as there is nothing contradictory in speaking of Winthrop's hair, now all gone, Winifred's flared trousers – they went up in flames years ago – and Wilfred's virginity lost only last night.

Objection 2: Dead people are not people (II).

The dead no longer exist; and so they cannot be affected by anything we now do – for good or ill. Further, as there is nothing in existence, there is nothing which should receive good treatment, even if we are unable to supply the treatment. When oysters have been eaten and digested, that's an end to those oysters (though maybe no end to the effects on us); and we cannot sensibly wonder whether those oysters are now tasty, best eaten with garlic or accompanied with champagne – or both.

Reply to Objection 2

Some will reject the objection, believing there is an afterlife. The Extensive Embrace demands no afterlife; so let us assume that death is annihilation. The mistake in the objection involves time. If Melissa kisses Miranda, then Melissa's kissing must occur when Miranda exists; but such examples do not justify the belief that, in all cases, when we affect items, there must be a time when the affecting actions and the items jointly exist. For example, actions can affect items – ones that are not yet in existence – through causal chains. Melissa's smoking might well affect the child yet to be conceived.

A revised belief is: for actions to affect items, either the actions, or some effects of the actions, must occur at some time during which the items affected exist. This revised belief is also false. Suppose that Melissa now, in 2004, believes that Cambridge will win the boat race in 2034. Whether she believes truly depends upon events in 2034, when she might well be dead. Indeed, suppose Winthrop dead: if someone, say, Melissa, now reading about him anew, comes to admire him, something has changed about Winthrop. At one stage, he was unadmired by Melissa; now he is admired. So, items can be affected by actions that occur after the items' existence, as well as before.

Objection 3: Death takes nothing away from the person who has died.

We speak of a person losing his life, but death can be no loss to the deceased – and so killing someone cannot be taking anything away from the deceased. Through death, the people who have died cease to exist and so suffer no loss; because of their death they never had that future life to lose.

Reply to Objection 3

This objection is akin to arguing that accidents cannot be prevented. If they are prevented, then they do not occur; and so there is nothing to prevent. When a death has occurred, the deceased no longer exists; so there is no loss that he has suffered. Accidents, though, can be prevented; for we can stop what would otherwise have occurred. Death is a loss, for it stops the future years of life that otherwise would have occurred for that individual. Hence, killing someone might well cause a significant loss to that individual and is one way in which we might mistreat an individual.

Objection 4: Mistreatment and good treatment require the recipients' awareness.

The changes identified in the *Reply to Objection 2* are all well and good – and labelled 'Cambridge changes' by Peter Geach, an important twentieth century philosopher – but the changes that someone undergoes when being treated well or badly involve more than that required by Cambridge changes. Whatever we do now will not benefit the dead, for beneficiaries need awareness of some effect for any benefits to occur. If we are thinking of the individuals right now, who no longer exist, there is no question of any awareness. If we are thinking of the individuals when they then lived, what we do now will not change their awareness one iota. Yes, we can make some of their past beliefs come true – yes, we can come to admire the deceased – but such changes can neither affect their awareness then nor now; hence, such changes have nothing to do with treating the deceased well or badly.

Reply to Objection 4

It is not true that good treatment and bad treatment can only occur if those individuals so treated have some awareness of some effects of the treatment. Air pollution might go unnoticed by us, yet still cause our premature death when asleep – a death that might be pretty bad for us. People who meet with accidents, causing them severe brain injuries, might then lead contented lives, unaware of all they have lost. They have still undergone severe losses and been harmed. Ask yourself whether you would really want to undergo such diminishment, even though you would be unaware of it as such.

Objection 5: Mistreatment and good treatment require the recipient's existence.

For changes to occur to individuals that are beneficial or harmful to them, the individuals need to exist – otherwise how can we make sense of their being benefited or harmed, well treated or badly treated?

Reply to Objection 5

Ah, yes, this is the crux; but why assume that actions *now* cannot benefit someone who once was? We should accept (from previous examples) that benefits can happen to individuals even though they are unaware of them – and that changes *now* can bring about changes to how individuals were, though without changing their then awareness. So what prevents the conjunction of those two factors? The answer might be based on the mistaken belief that benefits and harms require some change in the individual's body or consciousness; with the deceased, such changes can occur to them only when they lived – and anything we do now would require a backward causality to effect such changes. Events and actions, though, can affect individuals – can benefit or harm them – even though those events and actions occur far beyond the individuals' physical and psychological boundaries. Here are examples.

Mistreatment of living individuals can occur when we betray them or prevent them from achieving what they value or let them down by not following their wishes. These can be mistreatments, even if the victims cannot tell that they are being betrayed, thwarted or let down. Actions *now* can also affect how past lives stand by way of reputation, achievement and respect; hence, actions now can enhance or reduce that past life. This type of thinking – at least, partly – explains why we should often respect people's deathbed wishes, typically not lie about them after their death, and why we might promote what the deceased valued.

Objection 6: Concern for the deceased's reputation is mistaken for concern for the deceased.

Your examples show that we can harm the reputation and projects of the dead; we can fail to respect their memory – and so on. Such examples do not show that we are mistreating them.

Reply to Objection 6

Concern for a man's reputation is concern for the man. To think that they can come apart and should be valued separately is like saying that we never touch a person, but only the person's skin – and, thinking about it, we never really touch his skin, but only the skin's surface. Consider living persons: if we chop off their legs, ruin their reputations, betray their trust – if we damage their interests, mock their life's work and steal their cats – should we argue that, strictly speaking, we have not harmed them, but have instead mistreated their legs, reputations, trust – their interests, life's work and pets? Of course not – after all, we might even take loving care of the cats and the legs. The chopping, slander, betrayal – the damage, ridicule and theft – are ways in which we can harm living people; and there are similar ways in which we can harm dead people.

Objection 7: The argument fails to distinguish between direct and indirect treatment.

When we speak of treating people well or mistreating them, we typically have in mind direct treatment – not the indirect ones to do with damaging their reputation, values and pet goats. The dead cannot be mistreated in any direct way.

Reply to Objection 7

The demand that we should treat people well – the first premise of The Extensive Embrace – is one that covers both the direct and indirect modes mentioned. If you insist that treatment that benefits and harms individuals must be of the direct sort, then let us move to the following claim. What matters in our relationships with others is not just how we benefit and harm them, but also how we treat them indirectly; and, given this, it matters how we indirectly treat the dead as well as how we indirectly treat the living.

Objection 8: How we treat the dead is valuable solely because of the living.

The Extensive Embrace mistakenly identifies concern for how the living feel about treatment of the dead with concern for the dead. We pay attention to the deceased's will, his corpse and reputation because we do not want to upset those who live on.

Reply to Objection 8

Concern for the living is often a reason why we treat the dead as we do; but it does not prove that there is no concern for the deceased, independently of how the living are affected. If the living cared not about the treatment of the corpse and the deceased's deathbed wishes, the deceased could still have benefited from respect for his corpse and following his wishes. Further, that the living do mind about these matters might well indicate that they do mind how the deceased are treated for their (the deceased's) sake. It might also indicate that the living mind how they, in turn, will be treated, when deceased.

Objection 9: The Extensive Embrace slides us into slippery embraces.

If the argument is sound, we should find ourselves on slippery slopes into absurd concerns for non-existent people, for possible people and fictional characters.

Reply to Objection 9

The incantation 'slippery slope' on its own gets us nowhere (see 'Voluntary Sex' earlier in this collection). Whether there is a slippery slope, what sort of slope, and whether we should go down it – well, these are case by case matters. Concern for dead persons has a 'foothold in reality', to use an expression from Henry Salt – namely the real lives they once had. Salt was, by the way, an admirable late nineteenth century pioneer. Despite his privileged upbringing – Eton and King's, Cambridge – he spent much of his life arguing for humanitarianism, vegetarianism, animal rights and environmental conservation. Returning to reality's foothold, concern for future generations – or the child about to be conceived – also has a foothold, namely those individuals who will come about. So, there should be concern for these individuals; and people manifest this concern in various ecological – and even tax avoiding – ways. It does not follow that great-great-grandchildren yet to be born merit as much concern as children living today; one reason is that, for all we know, those great-great-grandchildren might not even come about and who knows what the then circumstances will be?

Turning to possible people and fictional characters, they simply lack any foothold in reality. That items have such footholds is essential for any (real) treatment of them to occur. This is not to say that there are no deep problems concerning the creation of people. If I could have created little Lizzie, but chose not to – have I harmed her?

There was, is, and will be no little Lizzie to have harmed – but perhaps that is the harm. Perhaps to think otherwise is to make a mistake not dissimilar from that which led to the conclusion that accidents cannot be prevented (see *Reply to Objection 3*).

Objection 10: The argument conceals important differences.

Whether one is quick or not – alive or dead – is morally significant. To suggest that the dead should be treated in the same way as the living is mad. We should be concerned far more about the living than the dead; so, even if the deceased really have interests, we should ignore them.

Reply to Objection 10

To suggest that the alive/dead status has no moral relevance would, indeed, be crazy. Treating the dead to bus passes, education and the right to vote, as we treat the living, would be silly. Thinking that ignoring someone's deathbed wishes is as bad as killing some trusting friends or torturing the cat is typically false. The Extensive Embrace is simply pointing out that there is such a thing as respecting the deceased, having concern for them – treating them well or badly. There is no suggestion that concern for the dead should usually be given as much weight as concern for the living.

Objection 11: The premise of The Extensive Embrace is faulty (I).

There are too many living people for us to treat well everyone who is living, let alone all the dead people. In fact, we should not even treat every living person well. Billions are unknown to us – and a few, such as criminals, deserve to be treated badly.

Reply to Objection 11

True, we cannot do everything that it would be good to do. Further, arguably, morality does not demand that we should all be saints. Perhaps we can agree on the more minimal claim that we ought not to treat people, including dead people, badly. If acceptance of our Extensive Embrace hangs on this matter, let us revise the embrace accordingly – into not treating people badly; and that includes not treating dead people badly.

That one should follow a certain moral principle typically has the caveat that, when it clashes with other moral principles, some further judgement is required over what one ought to do. The Extensive Embrace takes this background caveat as read. Now, if punishment counts as bad treatment, then, yes, criminals deserve to be treated badly. That would clash with the 'treating well' principle, but for the background caveat just mentioned.

Being dead itself, of course, is no crime; and we do not live in days when, for example, suicides – those who make themselves dead – are typically thought immoral. Further, there can be posthumous punishments. Consider how, in days long gone (at least in the UK), the more heinous crimes not merely led to hangings, but also to various disrespectful acts on the resultant corpses. This itself shows that dead people can be treated well, badly, justly and unjustly – by the way in the corpses are treated. The Extensive Embrace is making the point that in as far as people ought typically to be treated well or not treated badly, then so too dead people.

Objection 12: The premise of The Extensive Embrace is faulty (II).

Even if the argument is revised to speak of 'not harming' – and acknowledging the caveat about conflicting moral principles – we should recognize that some individuals have greater moral demands on us than others. Wondering – *purely impartially* – whether to save your child or someone else's is, arguably, itself immoral. Morality demands some partialities.

Reply to Objection 12

The Extensive Embrace need take no position on this. In as far as some partialities should take precedent over impartial treatment, this holds regarding our treatment of the dead. If – for example – we should sometimes favour friends over unknown individuals, then, in the spirit of the Extensive Embrace, we argue: we should treat friends well; therefore, we should treat dead friends well. As *Reply to Objection 10* made clear, no one is suggesting that concern for dead people always merits as much significance as concern for living people.

Objection 13: I remain unconvinced.

I can see the argument, but I cannot accept that I should have any concern for the deceased.

Reply to Objection 13

Although rationally we should typically adjust our beliefs to reason and evidence, we sometimes find ourselves unable so to do. 'A man convinced against his will is of the same opinion still' – Cardinal Newman's couplet might apply. Just because people assent to an argument's premises, follow the reasoning and believe that the conclusion should be accepted, it does not follow that they will believe the conclusion. Belief is not as immunized from will and desire as some would tell us. The objector's lack of conviction, even if accepting the argument as sound, manifests this psychological problem. This, though, is no objection to the argument. Perhaps such objectors should act as if the conclusion is true. Such acting might lead to genuine belief – and, in this case, true belief.

Until better objections are forthcoming, and, in paradoxical, albeit slightly revised, conclusion:

> *We ought not to harm people;*
> *Therefore, we ought not to harm those who no longer are people.*

That is, we ought not to harm dead people.

The Possibility of Life after Death

Richard Swinburne

In this paper I argue that a human on Earth consists of two interconnected parts (two substances, in philosophical terminology) – body and soul. The body is material; the soul is immaterial. The soul is the essential part of the person; it is the continuing of my soul which constitutes the continuing of me, as argued in my *The Evolution of the Soul*. At death my body ceases to function, and gradually decays. If there is a God, as I believe, what happens to the soul depends on his will; and I believe that he has revealed that normally he will keep it in existence forever. I do not know what would happen to the soul if there were no God. I can't prove to you in twenty minutes, as well as everything else, that there is a God and so that the soul will go on existing forever. But I can, I hope, prove to you that there is a soul for something to happen to.

I begin by introducing some philosophical terminology. I understand by a 'substance' a component of the world which interacts causally with other components of the world and which has a history through time. Tables and chairs, stars and galaxies, neurones, and persons are substances. Substances have intrinsic properties – such as being square or yellow, or having such and such an electric potential; they also have relational properties (properties which connect one substance with another), such as being taller than, or lying between. I understand by an 'event' the instantiation of a property in a particular substance or particular substances at particular times – such as this tie being now green, or this neurone firing at 3 p.m.; or Birmingham lying between London and Manchester in the last century. The history of the world is just the sequence of all the events which have happened. If you know all the events which have happened (which properties were instantiated in which substances and when), you know all that has happened.

Properties and events may be physical or mental. I shall understand by a 'physical property' one such that no one subject is necessarily better placed to know that it is instantiated than is any other subject. Physical properties are publicly accessible. Physical events are those which involve the instantiation of physical properties. This tie being green now is a physical event because not only am I able but anyone who wants to is equally able to find out the colour of my tie. Likewise, this neurone firing at 3 p.m. or John being now taller than George, are physical events. A mental property is one about which one person is necessarily in a better position to know than is anyone else. Mental events are events which involve the instantiation of mental properties. I understand by a 'material substance' one which occupies a region of space, and by an 'immaterial substance' one which does not occupy a space. Now, in the history of thought there have been three views on the mind/body problem, the problem of the relation between a human's mental life of thought and sensation, and the physical events in and around his body.

The first view, which I shall call 'hard materialism', claims that the only substances are material objects, and persons (including humans) are such substances. A person is the same thing as his body (and his brain is the same thing as his mind). The only events which occur are physical events, *viz*, ones which consist in the instantiation of physical properties in material objects. There are no mental events in the sense in which I have analysed this notion; for there are no events distinct from physical events to which the subject has privileged access. Hard materialism seems to me obviously false. There really are events which humans experience and which in consequence they can know about better than does anyone else who studies their behaviour or inspects their brain. My sensations – for example, my having a red after-image or a smell of roast beef – are such that I have an additional way of knowing about them other than those available to the best student of my behaviour or brain; I actually experience them. Consequently they must be distinct from brain events, or any other bodily events. A neurophysiologist cannot observe the quality of the colour in my visual field, or the pungency of the smell of roast beef which I smell. A Martian who came to Earth and captured a human being and inspected his brain, could discover everything that was happening in that brain but would still wonder whether a human really feels anything when his toe is stamped upon. There must be mental events in addition to physical events.

The second view in the history of thought about the mind/body problem is the view which I shall call 'soft materialism'. It is often called 'property dualism'. Soft materialism agrees with hard materialism that the only substances are material objects, but it claims that some of these (that is, persons) have mental properties which are distinct from physical properties. Brain-events certainly often cause mental events and vice versa. Neurones firing in certain patterns cause me to have a red after-image. And – and in the other direction – trying to move my arm causes the brain-events which cause my arm to move. These are causal relations between distinct events – just as the ignition of gunpowder is a distinct event from the explosion which it causes.

The basic difficulty, however, with soft materialism as with hard materialism, is that there seem to be more truths about the world than those allowed for by the doctrine. Hard materialism says that you have told the whole story of the world when you have said which material objects exist and which physical properties they have. But, as we have seen, there is also the issue of which mental properties are instantiated. Soft materialism says that you have told the whole story of the world when you have said which material objects exist and which properties (mental and physical) they have. However, full information of this kind would still leave you ignorant of whether some person continued to exist or not.

Knowledge of what happens to bodies and their parts will not show you for certain what happens to persons. Let me illustrate this with the example of brain transplants.

The brain, as you will know, consists of two hemispheres and a brain-stem. There is good evidence that humans can survive and behave as conscious beings if much of one hemisphere is destroyed. Now suppose my brain (hemispheres plus brain-stem) was divided into two, and each half brain taken out of my skull and transplanted into the empty skull of a body from which a brain has just been removed; and there to be added to each half-brain from some other brain (for example, the brain of my identical twin) whatever other parts (for example, more brain stem) are necessary in order for the transplant to take and for there to be two living persons with lives of conscious experiences. Which of these two resulting persons would be me? Probably both would, to some extent, behave like me and make my memory claims; for behaviour and speech depend, at any rate in very large part, on brain-states, and there is very considerable overlap between the 'information' carried by the two hemispheres which gives rise to behaviour and speech. But both persons would not be me. For if they were both identical with me they would be the same person as each other (if a is the same as b, and b is the same as c, then a is the same as c); yet they are not the same person. They now have different experiences and lead different lives. There remain three other possibilities – that the person with my right half-brain is me, or that the person with my left half-brain is me, or that neither is me. But we cannot be certain which holds. It follows that that mere knowledge of what happens to bodies does not tell you what happens to persons.

It is tempting to say that it is a matter of arbitrary definition which of the three possibilities is correct. But this temptation must be resisted. There is a crucial factual issue here – which can be shown if we alter our thought experiment a little. Suppose that I am captured by a mad surgeon. He explains that he is going to perform an operation on my brain, in consequence of which there will be two living persons, one made partly out of my right brain hemisphere and the other made partly out of my left brain hemisphere. He announces that he will give one of these later persons ten million dollars and that he will subject the other one to torture. He allows me to choose which of the later persons will get ten million dollars and which will be tortured; that is, to choose whether the person who has my left half-brain will become a rich man while the one who has my right half-brain will suffer, or whether it will be the other way around. How ought I to choose in order to become rich? It is evident that whether I shall survive the operation and whether my life will be happy or sad are factual questions. Only someone under the grip of some very strong philosophical dogma would deny that. They are factual questions, yet, as I await the transplant and know exactly what will happen to my brain, each of the two choices would be very risky. If I choose that the person with my left half-brain will be rewarded, I do not know whether it will be me; and also, if I choose that the person with my right half-brain will be rewarded, I do not know if that person will be me.

Even after the operation no one will know for certain whether I have survived, or which of the later persons is me. Even if one subsequent person resembles the earlier me more in character and memory claims than does the other, that one may not be me. Maybe I have survived the operation but am changed in character and have lost much of my memory as a result of it, in consequence of which the other subsequent person resembles the earlier me more in his public behaviour than I do. And even if a fourth possibility, that they are both to some extent me, were (despite its apparent incoherence) correct, neither science nor philosophy could show that to us for certain, for all the evidence which could ever be obtained would be compatible with the other possibilities as well.

Reflection on this thought experiment shows that however much we come to know about what has happened to my brain (and other parts of my body), and however much we come to know for certain about which mental properties are instantiated in which subsequent persons, we would not know for certain what has happened to me. What we would not know is which substance each of the later persons is. But since we do know – we may suppose – what has happened to each atom of my body, I must be different from my body. I must have a further essential immaterial part whose continuing in existence makes the brain (and so body) to which it is linked *my* brain (and *my* body), and to this something I give the traditional name of 'soul'. I am my soul plus whatever brain (and body) it is connected to. Normally my soul goes where my brain goes, but in unusual circumstances (such as when my brain is split) it is uncertain where it goes. And, I should add, it follows that it is uncertain whether it will return to the brain of my body, if it is frozen for one hundred years (and inevitably damaged by the freezing process) – someone may come to life when my body is unfrozen, but it may not be me.

There is a fashionable way of attempting to avoid this conclusion by pointing out that we do not always know the essence of that which we pick out by our referring expressions. The early Greeks called the planet which appeared in the evening sky 'Hesperus', and the planet which appeared in the morning sky 'Phosphorus', but they did not know that these planets were the same planet. In their ignorance they would then have supposed various suppositions to be coherent which in fact would be metaphysically impossible, that is, impossible for the same reason as that it is impossible that a self-contradiction be true – for example, Hesperus and Phosphorus being totally present in different regions of the sky at the same time. Might it not be the case, similarly, that we do not know to what we are referring by 'I' or 'Swinburne'? And that in fact we are referring to a certain part of the brain – let's say the pineal gland. Maybe I am my pineal gland, and science will eventually discover this. The comparison of this to the situation of Hesperus and Phosphorus is not, however, apt. Certain words are indeed used without a full understanding of what is being referred to, but for the words to have a meaning there has to be an understanding of the kind of thing being referred to and what constitutes that thing continuing to exist – and so what science would need to discover in order to discover that a future object was that object. The Greeks used 'Hesperus' to refer to a material object, and understood that continuing to exist would amount to the matter of which Hesperus was made continuing to exist stuck together (spatio-temporal continuity being evidence of sameness of matter). However the split brain experiment brings out that 'I' and 'Swinburne' are <u>not</u> used to pick out a material object, such as the pineal gland. For if they were, knowledge of what happened to all the atoms of my body (plus the mental properties associated therewith) would entail a conclusion about what happened to me, in the way that knowledge of what has happened to all the atoms of Hesperus entails a conclusion about what has happened to Hesperus. But knowledge of what has happened to all the atoms of my body, etc., does not entail that – as has been shown.

Nor is any of the matter of my present brain (metaphysically) necessary for my present existence. For clearly the world could (it is metaphysically possible that it should) have been different in the respect that, while just the same pattern of physical and mental properties were instantiated (and so someone with just this kind of body talked to an audience with just these kinds of bodies), one of you could have had my body and I could have had yours. A full description of the world would need to include a description not merely of what bodies there were, but of who had them; and that means a fully non-bodily 'who'. The concept of me is the concept of a soul. Undoubtedly I exist and so there is something satisfying that concept. I am essentially a soul, an immaterial substance distinct from my body. Hence, at death, when the soul is separated from the body, it is possible that it continues to exist. So, if there is a God, he can, if he so wishes, make it continue to exist either on its own or by connecting it again to its old body or to a new body, if its previous body has been annihilated.

Reply to Richard Swinburne

Hugh Mellor

Richard Swinburne's thesis starts with the claim that everyone alive has two important parts, a body and a soul (the soul I shall call the 'mind', since for present purposes it doesn't matter which we call it, and I don't want to take advantage of any irrelevantly controversial implications of the term 'soul'). The difference between these two parts is that the mind is the part of a person which has his or her mental properties, these for Richard being the properties that at any one time are best known to the person whose mind it is: typically, states of consciousness.

Given these assumptions, Richard then claims that these two parts of an embodied person can exist separately. Now with half of this claim we can all agree: namely that Richard's body could exist without a mind. For, when he dies, that is what his corpse is – a body without a mind – and this we can all agree will not be Richard. For Richard to survive it is not enough for his body to survive.

The question then is whether the *other* part of Richard, his mind, can exist apart from his body; and whether, if it does so, that part of him *is* Richard, or is something else again. Richard says that is possible; I say it isn't, in any serious sense of possibility.

Richard's case for the possibility of our surviving as disembodied minds rests on an argument about our identity over time. This argument takes the form of a thought-experiment in which a person – Richard, for example – is duplicated in the way he describes. Richard then assumes that there must be an answer to the question of which of the two people who emerge from this experiment will be him: the possible answers being that one of them is and the other isn't, or that neither of them is. And from this he concludes that there must be something, not entailed by any facts about Richard's body, which determines whether Richard has continued to exist and, if he does, which of the two later people he is.

I think several things are right about this argument. I'm sure that anyone faced with Richard's awful prospect will think that there *is* an answer to these questions, even if it isn't obvious what the answer is. In this particular case I'm inclined to think that *neither* of the two people resulting from Richard's duplication is Richard. Take Richard's Hesperus/Phosphorus analogue, and imagine that planet being split into two parts, each of which then grows by accretion until there are two planets just like the original. We would then face the same question: what, if anything, tells you which if either of the two planets you now have is the one you started with?

It seems to me as obvious here as in Richard's duplication example that nothing about the original entity, whether it be a planet or a person, tells us the answer to that question. Yet the issue in the planet case cannot be settled by crediting the planet with an identity-carrying mind. Why then should that be what settles it when people are duplicated? Surely the answer, whatever it is, must be the same in both cases.

Note also that Richard only gave us three options in his duplication example: namely, that after the operation either one of the two embodied characters is Richard, or the other one is, or Richard ceases to exist. Why did he not raise the possibility, if neither of those two embodied people is Richard, that Richard has floated off on his own in some disembodied way? The reason surely is that nothing in his story even begins to suggest that you can have a person who *isn't* embodied. There may well be hard questions about *which* past embodied person a presently embodied person is, but that's a question about what determines the identity over time of embodied people. The difficulty of these questions does nothing to show that we can exist *without* being embodied, which is what Richard needs in order to show that we could survive the death and destruction of our bodies.

And once we see this, it seems clear to me that all the evidence we *do* have suggests that our minds depend on our bodies (including our brains). There are many obvious interactions between our mental and our bodily properties. These interactions admittedly go both ways, since conscious experiences can have physical effects, as when embarrassment makes you blush, just as physical causes can have mental effects, as when photons entering your eyes cause you to see me. You don't have to be a materialist – i.e. to think that all mental states *are* physical – to admit that our mental properties depend on our physical ones. You can think, as I do, that we have properties which do not reduce to physical properties, and still acknowledge that not only the nature but the very existence of our conscious experiences depends on our having bodies. All the evidence of our own and other people's lives overwhelmingly implies this.

Next I'd like to comment briefly on Richard's unusually narrow characterisation of mental properties. I don't think that this matters much to his argument, but it may affect its appeal. The point is that some properties which most people would call mental are *not* necessarily best known to the people whose properties they are. Think for example of the subconscious or unconscious states of mind postulated by Freudian and other psychologists. Or take the many less controversial states which are normally counted as mental, but which also need not fit Richard's definition, such as your beliefs, your desires, your intentions.

Several theories of the mind strongly suggest that other people may know as well as you do whether you are in some of these seemingly mental states. And on these theories we need a body to *be* in many of these states, since they entail dispositions to behave in ways in which only bodies *can* behave. How, for example, can you be disposed to go home after this meeting, if you have no body to take you there? In short, as generally understood, mentality covers many traits that are important to our character, and to our human capacities, which you couldn't have without a body: not just as a matter of causation, but because you *need* a body in order to have those traits.

My other comment on Richard's definition of mental properties is this. It may be necessary to our concepts of some mental states that only their owners can know directly that they are in them. But we may still have a perfectly good physical explanation of this so-called privileged access which embodied people have to those states. For we can, and I believe we do, have internal senses which make us aware of states that we are in which other people cannot detect in us, or at least not detect in the same way. That moreover is a feature which could be built into something that isn't mental at all: for example, there can be self-scanning devices within a machine which monitor the machine's internal states and whose output is used by the machine itself (e.g. to repair damage), yet those internal states need not be physically accessible to anything outside that machine. I see no mystery, nor anything essentially mental, in such privileged access.

None of these however is the main point I wish to make, which is simply that I see nothing in Richards's argument which shows that mental properties, even of his limited sort, can be possessed by anything which does not have a body.

Two final comments. First, the fact that you can *imagine* a mind without a body doesn't show that it's *possible* for minds to exist without bodies. It's too easy to imagine (or think we imagine) things that we know to be impossible. For example, (I think) I can imagine there being a greatest prime number – i.e. a number which can only be divided by itself and one, such that no greater number can also be divided only by itself and one. Yet I know and understand the well-known proof that there is no such number. So, imaginability, or apparent conceivability, does not seem to me a strong argument even for logical possibility. And second, even if we grant that it's *logically* possible for our minds to survive bodily death, just as it's logically possible for pigs to fly, that doesn't show that it's *physically* possible. It may still follow from laws of nature that in order to have any of Richard's mental properties, you need a physical body. That seems to me strongly implied by all the evidence we have about how our mental states depend on our bodily states. In other words, even if it is not merely apparently conceivable but logically possible for us to survive bodily death, we still have every reason to think that it is not physically possible for us to do so.

An Afterlife

A Disembodied Life?

Anthony Flew

> *'...Who would fardels bear,*
> *To grunt and sweat under a weary life,*
> *But that the dread of something after death,*
> *The undiscover'd country, from whose bourn*
> *No traveller returns, puzzles the will,*
> *And makes us rather bear those ills we have*
> *Than fly to others that we know not of?*
> *Thus conscience doth make cowards of us all...'*
>
> Shakespeare, *Hamlet*, I, iii.

It was to the fact of this conscience, in the sense of consciousness, that Einstein was referring when he remarked, in a conversation with Herbert Feigl, 'If there were not this internal illumination, then the Universe would be a mere rubbish heap'[1]. In discussing the subject of this collection of papers we must never forget that, until the beginnings of modern science, absolutely everyone believed that the Universe was full of incorporeal spirits endowed with active powers. Such spirits were ill-equipped to serve as the hypothetical entities of an explanatory theory. For no one was able to propose any way in which they might have been identified with reference to the movements which they had been introduced to explain. Nor, once such a hypothesis has been adopted, are there are any fresh and testable inferences to be drawn from it. It is worth noting here an illuminating comment by an historian of the origins of modern science:

> 'The modern law of inertia, the modern theory of motion, is the great factor which in the seventeenth century helped to drive the spirits out of the world... Not only so – but the very first men who in the middle ages launched the great attack on the Aristotelian theory were conscious of the fact that this colossal issue was involved in the question... Jean Buridan in the fourteenth century pointed out that his first alternative theory would eliminate the need for the Intelligences that turned the celestial spheres. He even noted that the Bible provided no authority for these agencies...'[2]

---

[1] Recorded in K. R. Popper and J.C. Eccles *The Self and its Brain* (Berlin, New York and London: Springer, 1997).
[2] Herbert Butterfield *The Origins of Modern Science* (London: G. Bell 1951), pp6-7. Herbert Butterfield was an active member of the Methodist chapel which I attended as a youth with my parents.

But it appears to have been several centuries before this elimination of the conception or misconception of incorporeal agent spirits from classical mechanics began to have any effect either on the philosophy of mind or on the philosophy of religion, at least in the English-speaking philosophical world. Indeed, until the publication of Gilbert Ryle's *The Concept of the Mind,* the standard work on the philosophy of mind, to which the students were routinely referred, was C.D. Broad's *The Mind and its Place in Nature.* Broad himself was much interested in, and later published a volume of his own essays about, psychical research[1]. That discipline at that time (which was before its development into parapsychology) was mainly concerned with mediumistic communications to and from the putatively surviving spirits of dead persons. But, so far as I know, no one in those far off pre-Rylean days ever challenged the legitimacy of the concept of the surviving spirit of a dead person.

I trust that my age will excuse me for introducing here one or two personal reminiscences of how things were in British philosophy fifty and more years ago. For it happens that I was a graduate student working under Ryle during the calendar year in which *The Concept of Mind* was first published. In that work Ryle's fundamental contention was that the word 'mind' is not a word for an entity which could significantly be said to survive the death and dissolution of the flesh and blood person whose mind it had been. For – and Ryle himself would have enjoyed putting the matter in this way – to construe the question whether she has a mind of her own as a question about an hypothesized incorporeal substance would be like taking the loss of the Red Queen's dog's temper as if it was on all fours with the loss of its bone, or like looking for the grin remaining after the Cheshire Cat itself had disappeared.

So far as I know Ryle never expressed any view on the question of a future life. But I do remember watching, as a graduate student, his obviously distasteful shelving of a copy of *The Concept of Soul,* a volume in the same format, and from the same publisher, as *The Concept of Mind.* This volume had presumably come into his hands in his capacity as Editor of the philosophy journal *Mind*, and it was certainly never reviewed in that journal.

A few years later when I confided in Ryle my intention, if I was ever invited to give the Gifford Lectures, to give them on 'The Logic of Mortality', he expressed neither agreement nor disagreement. I had, and have, little doubt but that he did agree with me concerning these matters. But he was then, as always, careful not to say anything which might, as so many things did, attract hostile media attention to 'Oxford linguistic philosophy'.

Turning now to Richard Swinburne's paper, 'The Possibility of Life after Death', we find

---

[1] C.D. Broad *Lectures on Psychical Research* (New York: Humanities, 1962).

that he begins by claiming that a human on Earth consists of two interconnected parts (two substances in philosophical terminology) – body and soul. The body is material, the soul is immaterial. The soul is the essential part of the person; it is the continuing of my soul which constitutes the continuing of me.

Swinburne concludes this initial paragraph by expressing the hope that he can, in his paper, 'prove to you that there is a soul for something to happen to'.

What is so very remarkable is that Swinburne should have hoped to establish this conclusion without attempting to explain either how individual spiritual substances are to be identified in the first place or later re-identified as the same individual spiritual substances. Instead, after first disposing of 'hard materialism', as he terms it, he attempts to dispose of 'soft materialism'. Soft materialism, for Swinburne, says that you have told the whole story of the world when you have said what material objects exist and which properties (mental and physical) they have; however, full information of this kind would still leave one ignorant of whether some person continued to exist or not; knowledge of what happens to bodies and their parts will not show you for certain what happens to persons.

By way of reply, I say that, on the contrary, until and unless you have introduced and justified a new usage of the word 'person' in which a person may be either a kind of creature of flesh and blood or a kind of incorporeal spiritual being, you will have to admit that, if the body of a flesh and blood person shows all the usual indices of death, then that person is unequivocally dead; and, as so being, must necessarily lack mental properties.

My own first approach to the question of a future life was indirect, making no reference to death or its possible consequences. It took the form of a paper on 'Locke and the Problem of Personal Identity', published in *Philosophy* 1951. In it, accepting Bishop Butler's demonstration that memory can reveal but cannot constitute personal identity[1], I proceeded to insist that people are a very special sort of creature of flesh and blood and bones. Hence the incorrigibly decisive, if usually impracticable, way to establish that the prisoner in the dock is the same as the person who did the deed would be to demonstrate in complete detail the route taken by the doer of the deed from the time of the doing until the time of entering the dock. Given this, the most which the most brilliant and expensive defence counsel could hope to do would be to maintain either that there were extenuating circumstances or that the prisoner had suffered a psychological transformation such that he or she no longer possessed a *mens rea*.

---

[1] Curiously, Richard Swinburne made no mention of this demonstration in at least the first edition of his *The Evolution of the Soul*

That same, now ancient, paper of mine also contained a less surgical anticipation of Swinburne's example of the mad surgeon and his separation of someone's left hemisphere from their right hemisphere. My supposition was that someone had split like an amoeba into two people; my contention was that there would be no antecedently correct answer to the question which of the two amoebae after the split would be the same one as the single amoeba before the split. The case would generate one of those legal cases in which a predicament which had not been foreseen by the original legislators required later lawyers to decide what future legally correct usage was to be. I believe that I referred to an actual twentieth century case in which a Court had to decide whether, under a law introduced in an earlier century, a flying boat was or was not a ship. The case imagined by Swinburne, if it actually arose, would properly have to have a similar procedure to reach a decision.

The relevance of all this reminiscence is to help readers to realize that Swinburne has not succeeded in his attempt to prove that 'there is a soul for something to happen to'. So long as we think of people or persons as members of a kind of creatures of flesh and blood, then everyone knows how to establish that there is a person at the front door, whatever difficulties there may sometimes be or have been in identifying or reidentifying him or her as one particular person. And we have already indicated here, the proper principles for the reidentification of one and the same person after what the lawyers call 'an effluxion of time'.

But neither Swinburne nor, so far as I know, anyone else has ever succeeded in showing how an individual could be identified as a substance, much less reidentified as one and the same substance after an effluxion of time.

In his recent article on 'Gods, Ghosts and Curious Persons'[1] John Gaskin has extended this critique of the idea of incorporeal personal agents to the idea of God, as defined by Swinburne:

> *'The original point of departure was that in the historically dominant and all but irreducible minimum understanding of what God is (and must be) to a Jew, Christian or Muslim, God is always spoken about, and spoken to, as a sort of person; a person moreover who is emphatically not pure mind, but who also acts; who is an agent without a body ('without body, parts of passions' in the Anglican formula), who is always able to do anything anywhere.'*

---

[1] Published as 'Guest Article' in *Philosophical Writings*, No. 13, Spring 2000. The passage quoted is on page 73.

The tension here is obvious. Body acts are carried out by persons acting with their own bodies. All that a person can do or bring about in the physical world consists in, or is an indirect act resulting from, such direct acts. The absence of a body is therefore not only factual grounds for doubting whether a person exists – there's no one there! It is also grounds for doubting whether such a bodiless entity could possibly be an agent.

Finally, I want to insist that in any discussion of the philosophical question of a future life we should always remember that, as Sartre once insisted, 'in religion there are also the damned'. If there are, and we are substantial and hence possibly surviving souls, we humanists will have to do a lot of rethinking.

The Gambler's Argument: Blaise Pascal

Nigel Warburton

Imagine you are on your death bed. You have been an agnostic all your adult life, but are now aware that you have at best a few hours to live. You still believe that there is a small chance that the Christian God exists; that is why you never felt able to embrace atheism and declare that there is no God. But you are not convinced that there is a God. In fact on balance you believe there is no God, no heaven, no hell, and that within a few hours you will simply cease to exist forever, except in other people's memories and by the other traces you have left behind you. At this moment, a friend who has read Blaise Pascal's *Pensées* comes in and tries to persuade you to embrace a belief in God.

You: I really think this is it. I have to be honest with you, I don't think I'll last much longer.

She: Don't speak like that, you could still recover.

You: No. I've spoken to two doctors now. They only give me a matter of hours. I'm about to slip away to nothing. I can't say I feel too bad about it. Perhaps it's the painkillers I'm on, but I feel quite serene. I've been lucky, I've had quite a good life. Plenty of friends, no serious hardships. Why are you crying? Don't cry. Let's talk about something else. Look out of the window, the crocuses have come out already. It's not that bad.

She: It might be.

You: What do you mean? Why are you looking so scared?

She: What if you are wrong? What if Hell really exists and you end up there forever?

You: But it probably doesn't exist, does it. Be realistic. It doesn't seem very likely. You've been looking at too many Hieronymous Bosch paintings…Hell is a medieval belief. We're in the twenty-first century.

She: Look, don't you understand – if there's only a tiny chance that Hell exists and you might end up there boiling in sulphur with little devils jabbing at you with tridents for eternity, it's worth trying to avoid, isn't it?

You: I don't get your drift.

She: Look, what would it cost you now to start believing in God?

You: Well, I don't believe God exists. But I'm happy to admit I don't know for sure that he doesn't. No one does.

She: Answer my question: what would it *cost* you?

You: Not a lot I suppose, except my integrity in my last few hours. I can't just believe something I don't really believe.

She: Let's suppose you're right that God probably doesn't exist. You haven't ever really believed that he did, so it won't be a big surprise, nasty or otherwise for you.

You: It won't be a surprise at all as I won't be there to have the surprise.

She: I don't want to quibble now, but it *is possible* that there is no God *and* that we survive our deaths…you don't have to believe in a God to believe in an afterlife, but it probably helps.

You: OK, fair point, but where are you going with this?

She: What I mean is that you won't have gained or lost much if you choose to believe and it so happens there isn't a God.

You: I suppose I'll have gained the knowledge that my informed guess was right. But actually, come to think of it, I probably won't be there to feel smug. So it's not obvious that I'll have gained anything, I agree. Except, from an objective perspective, I'll have lived out my life in a way that is consistent with what really exists. I won't have been duped. That can't be bad.

She: Yes, but think of what it will be like if God does exist, and that the only route to avoiding Hell is to believe in him…

You: Then I'll have blown it.

She: Yes, but on a spectacular scale. You'll have thrown away the chance of everlasting bliss, and had everlasting torment as the consolation prize. You haven't got much time, so I'll put this as forcefully as I can. I love you. I don't want anything bad to happen to you. What you should try and do is think of this as a gamble. Play to maximise your winnings and minimise your losses. There is a lot at stake here. If you get it wrong, you get eternal damnation; but if you get it right, eternal bliss. It seems to me that by opting to sit on the fence and die an agnostic you won't have a chance of the big pay out, but you'll also run the risk of the worst possible scenario. Why would any sane person do that? Please take me seriously. How can you raise your eyebrow at me like that at this time?

You: OK, let's say that I accept your gamble and opt to believe in God – and by the way, I read Pascal years ago when I was at college, so I know where you're coming from. But I'd still be left with the problem: How do I go about believing in something I don't really believe in. I can't just say 'Abracadabra' and then find myself believing in God, can I? Actually, I find the Problem of Evil – that there exists so much suffering in the world – rather persuasive as an argument *against* the existence of God…

She: You've obviously forgotten Pascal's answer about how to believe what you don't really believe. He says, more or less, do what believers do outwardly, and pretty soon you'll get the internal belief that goes with the behaviour. What starts off as an act will become sincere. It's like method acting in reverse. Instead of going for the motivation and finding its outward expression, just imitate the outer and you'll get the inner….Pascal talks about praying, taking communion, that sort of thing.

You: It all seems a bit late for that. That's all a bit close to a death-bed conversion for me.

She: Well you could say a prayer with me…

You: Didn't you read William James as well?

She: What?

You: As I remember it, he said that, if he were God, he'd take great delight in consigning anyone who believed in him on the basis of Pascal's Wager to eternal damnation! Believing in God on the selfish grounds that it seems like a good gamble surely has to be all wrong. I rather hope that a good God, if he exists, won't mind letting the odd honest agnostic in, in preference to self-interested gamblers. Anyway, if I went down the route you're suggesting, I'd have to try believing not just in the Christian God, but in the God of Islam, the Hindu gods, and a whole range of other ones too, just in case any of them exists. I don't think I could cope with all that. Not when I'm feeling so weak. I tell you what – I'm getting a bit sleepy now with all this philosophising. Why don't you say a prayer for me, if it makes you feel better, while I try and think up something witty to say as my last words. Oh, don't start crying again…

The Death of David Hume

Letter From Adam Smith, LL.D.

to

William Strachan, Esq.

Kirkaldy, Fifeshire, Nov. 9, 1776.

DEAR SIR,— It is with a real, though a very melancholy pleasure, that I sit down to give some account of the behavior of our late excellent friend, Mr. Hume, during his last illness.

Though, in his own judgment, his disease was mortal and incurable, yet he allowed himself to be prevailed upon, by the entreaty of his friends, to try what might be the effects of a long journey. A few days before he set out, he wrote that account of his own life, which, together with his other papers, he has left to your care. My account, therefore, shall begin where his ends.

He set out for London towards the end of April, and at Morpeth met with Mr. John Home and myself, who had both come down from London on purpose to see him, expecting to have found him at Edinburgh. Mr. Home returned with him, and attended him during the whole of his stay in England, with that care and attention which might be expected from a temper so perfectly friendly and affectionate. As I had written to my mother that she might expect me in Scotland, I was under the necessity of continuing my journey. His disease seemed to yield to exercise and change of air, and when he arrived in London, he was apparently in much better health than when he left Edinburgh. He was advised to go to Bath to drink the waters, which appeared for some time to have so good an effect upon him, that even he himself began to entertain, what he was not apt to do, a better opinion of his own health. His symptoms, however, soon returned with their usual violence, and from that moment he gave up all thoughts of recovery, but submitted with the utmost cheerfulness, and the most perfect complacency and resignation.

Upon his return to Edinburgh, though he found himself much weaker, yet his cheerfulness never abated, and he continued to divert himself, as usual, with correcting his own works for a new edition, with reading books of amusement, with the conversation of his friends; and, sometimes in the evening, with a party at his favorite game of whist. His cheerfulness was so great, and his conversation and amusements run so much in their usual strain, that, notwithstanding all bad symptoms, many people could not believe he was dying. 'I shall tell your friend, Colonel Edmondstone,' said Doctor Dundas to him one day, 'that I left you much better, and in a fair way of recovery.' 'Doctor,' said he, 'as I believe you would not choose to tell any thing but the truth, you had better tell him, that I am dying as fast as my enemies, if I have any, could wish, and as easily and cheerfully as my best friends could desire.' Colonel Edmondstone soon afterwards came to see him, and take leave of him; and on his way home, he could not forbear writing him a letter bidding him once more an eternal adieu, and applying to him, as to a dying man, the beautiful French verses in which the Abbé Chaulieu, in expectation of his own death, laments his approaching separation from his friend, the Marquis de la Fare.

Mr. Hume's magnanimity and firmness were such, that his most affectionate friends knew that they hazarded nothing in talking or writing to him as to a dying man, and that so far from being hurt by this frankness, he was rather pleased and flattered by it. I happened to come into his room while he was reading this letter, which he had just received, and which he immediately showed me. I told him, that though I was sensible how very much he was weakened, and that, appearances were in many respects very bad, yet his cheerfulness was still so great, the spirit of life seemed still to be so very strong in him, that I could not help entertaining some faint hopes. He answered, 'Your hopes are groundless. An habitual diarrhoea of more than a year's standing, would be a very bad disease at any age: at my age it is a mortal one. When I lie down in the evening, I feel myself weaker than when I rose in the morning; and when I rise in the morning, weaker than when I lay down in the evening. I am sensible, besides, that some of my vital parts are affected, so that I must soon die.' 'Well,' said I, 'if it must be so, you have at least the satisfaction of leaving all your friends, your brother's family in particular, in great prosperity.' He said that he felt that satisfaction so sensibly, that when he was reading, a few days before, Lucian's Dialogues of the Dead, among all the excuses which are alleged to Charon for not entering readily into his boat, he could not find one that fitted him; he had no house to finish, he had no daughter to provide for, he had no enemies upon whom he wished to revenge himself. 'I could not well imagine,' said he, 'what excuse I could make to Charon in order to obtain a little delay. I have done every thing of consequence which I ever meant to do; and I could at no time expect to leave my relations and friends in a better situation than that in which I am now likely to leave them. I therefore have all reason to die contented.' He then diverted himself with inventing several jocular excuses, which he supposed he might make to Charon, and with imagining the very surly answers which it might suit the character of Charon to return to them. 'Upon further consideration,' said he, 'I thought I might say to him, Good Charon, I have been correcting my works for a new edition. Allow me a little time, that I may see how the public receives the alterations.' But Charon would answer, 'When you have seen the effect of these, you will be for making other alterations. There will be no end of such excuses; so, honest friend, please step into the boat.' But I might still urge, 'Have a little patience, good Charon; I have been endeavoring to open the eyes of the public. If I live a few years longer, I may have the satisfaction of seeing the downfall of some of the prevailing systems of superstition.' But Charon would then lose all temper and decency. 'You loitering rogue, that will not happen these many hundred years. Do you fancy I will grant you a lease for so long a term? Get into the boat this instant, you lazy loitering rogue.'

But, though Mr. Hume always talked of his approaching dissolution with great cheerfulness, he never affected to make any parade of his magnanimity. He never mentioned the subject but when the conversation naturally led to it, and never dwelt longer upon it than the course of the conversation happened to require: it was a subject, indeed, which occurred pretty frequently, in consequence of the inquiries which his friends, who came to see him, naturally made concerning the state of his health. The conversation which I mentioned above, and which passed on Thursday the 8th of August, was the last, except one, that I ever had with him.

He had now become so very weak, that the company of his most intimate friends fatigued him; for his cheerfulness was still so great, his complaisance and social disposition were still so entire, that when any friend was with him, he could not help talking more, and with greater exertion, than suited the weakness of his body. At his own desire, therefore, I agreed to leave Edinburgh, where I was staying partly upon his account, and returned to my mother's house here, at Kirkaldy, upon condition that he would send for me whenever he wished to see me; the physician who saw him most frequently, Dr. Black, undertaking, in the mean time, to write me occasionally an account of the state of his health.

On the 22d of August, the Doctor wrote me the following letter:

> 'Since my last, Mr. Hume has passed his time pretty easily, but is much weaker. He sits up, goes down stairs once a day, and amuses himself with reading, but seldom sees anybody. He finds that even the conversation of his most intimate friends fatigues and oppresses him; and it is happy that he does not need it, for he is quite free from anxiety, impatience, or low spirits, and passes his time very well with the assistance of amusing books.'

I received the day after a letter from Mr. Hume himself, of which the following is an extract:

> *Edinburgh, 23d August, 1776.*
>
> 'MY DEAREST FRIEND,—I am obliged to make use of my nephew's hand in writing to you, as I do not rise today.
> *   *   *   *   *   *   *   *   *   *
> I go very fast to decline, and last night had a small fever, which I hoped might put a quicker period to this tedious illness, but unluckily it has, in a great measure, gone off. I cannot submit to your coming over here on my account, as it is possible for me to see you so small a part of the day, but Doctor Black can better inform you concerning the degree of strength which may from time to time remain with me. Adieus etc.'

Three days after I received the following letter from Doctor Black:

Edinburgh, Monday, 26th August, 1776.

'DEAR SIR,—Yesterday, about four o'clock, afternoon, Mr. Hume expired. The near approach of his death became evident in the night between Thursday and Friday, when his disease became excessive, and soon weakened him so much that he could no longer rise out of his bed. He continued to the last perfectly sensible, and free from much pain or feelings of distress. He never dropped the smallest expression of impatience; but when he had occasion to speak to the people about him, always did it with affection and tenderness. I thought it improper to write to bring you over, especially as I heard that he had dictated a letter to you desiring you not to come. When he became very weak, it cost him an effort to speak, and he died in such a happy composure of mind, that nothing could exceed it.'

Thus died our most excellent and never to be forgotten friend; concerning whose philosophical opinions men will, no doubt, judge variously, every one approving or condemning them, according as they happen to coincide or disagree with his own; but concerning whose character and conduct there can scarce be a difference of opinion. His temper, indeed, seemed to be more happily balanced, if I may be allowed such an expression, than that perhaps of any other man I have ever known. Even in the lowest state of his fortune, his great and necessary frugality never hindered him from exercising, upon proper occasions, acts both of charity and generosity. It was a frugality founded, not upon avarice, but upon the love of independency. The extreme gentleness of his nature never weakened either the firmness of his mind or he steadiness of his resolutions. His constant pleasantry was the genuine effusion of good nature and good humour, tempered with delicacy and modesty, and without even the slightest tincture of malignity, so frequently the disagreeable source of what is called wit in other men. It never was the meaning of his raillery to mortify; and, therefore, far from offending, it seldom failed to please and delight, even those who were the objects of it. To his friends, who were frequently the objects of it, there was not perhaps any one of all his great and amiable qualities, which contributed more to endear his conversation. And that gaiety of temper, so agreeable in society, but which is so often accompanied with frivolous and superficial qualities, was in him certainly attended with the most severe application, the most extensive learning, the greatest depth of thought, and a capacity in every respect the most comprehensive. Upon the whole, I have always considered him, both in his lifetime and since his death, as approaching as nearly to the idea of a perfectly wise and virtuous man, as perhaps the nature of human frailty will permit.

I am ever, dear Sir
Most affectionately yours,
ADAM SMITH.

Further Readings

General

Everitt, Nicholas, *The Non-Existence of God* (Routledge, 2003)

Hanfling, O. (ed), *Life and Meaning* (Blackwell, 1987)

Harris, John, *Bioethics* (OUP, 2001)

Harris, John, *The Value of Life: Introduction to Medical Ethics* (Routledge, 1985)

Nagel, T., *What does it all mean?* (Oxford University Press, 1987)

Williams, B., *Problems of the Self* (Cambridge University Press, 1973)

Introduction

Miller, Stephen, 'The Death of Hume', *Wilson Quarterly* 3039 (Summer 1995)

Six Months to Live

LeBon, T., *Wise Therapy* (Sage 2001)

Marinoff, L., *Plato Not Prozac!* (Harper Collins, 1999)

Nagel, T., *Mortal Questions* (Cambridge University Press, 1979)

Nagel, T., *What does it all mean?* (Oxford University Press, 1987)

Robinson, R., *An Atheist's Values* (Blackwell, 1964, out of print, or http://www.positiveatheism.org/hist/athval0.htm)

Williams, B., *Problems of the Self* (Cambridge University Press, 1973)

Intimations of Immortality

Bodnar, A.G., Ouellette, M., Frolkis, M., Holt, S. E., Chiu, C. P., Morin, G. B., Harley, C. B., Shay, J. W., Lichtsteiner, S., Wright, W. E., 'Extension of life-span by introduction of telomerase into normal human cells', *Science,* Vol.279, No.5349, pp.349-352 (1998)

Dworkin, Ronald, *Life's Dominion*, p. 148 on procreative liberty (Harper Collins, 1993)

European Convention on Human Rights, Article 8 and Article 12 (1953)

Harris, John, 'QALYfying The Value of Life', *Journal of Medical Ethics,* 117-123 (September, 1987)

Harris, John, 'What the principal objective of the NHS should *really* be', *The British*

Medical Journal 314 (1ˢᵗ March 1997. 669-672)

Harris, John, 'Genes, Clones and Human Rights' in Justine C. Burley Ed. *The Genetic Revolution and Human Rights: The Amnesty Lectures 1998* (Oxford University Press, 1999)

Harris, John, 'Rights and Reproductive Choice' in John Harris and Søren Holm Eds. *The Future of Human Reproduction: Choice and Regulation* (Oxford University Press. 1998)

Harris, John, *Wonderwoman & Superman: The Ethics of Human Biotechnology,* Chapters 2 and 3 (Oxford University Press, 1992)

International Covenant of Civil and Political Rights, Article 23 (1976)

Lanza, R. P., Cibelli, J. B., West, M. D., 'Prospects for the use of nuclear transfer in human transplantation', *Nature Biotechnology*, Vol.17, No.12, pp.1171-1174 (1999)

Lanza, R. P., Cibelli, J. B., West, M. D., 'Human therapeutic cloning', *Nature Medicine,* Vol.5, No.9, pp.975-977 (1999)

McBrearty, B. A., Clark, L. D., Zhang-X. M., Blankenhorn, E. P., Heber-Katz, E., 'Genetic analysis of a mammalian wound-healing trait' *Proceedings Of The National Academy Of Sciences Of The United States Of America,* 95(20): 11792-7 (1998 Sep 29)

McKie, John, Richardson, Jeff, Singer, Peter & Kuhse, Helga, *The Allocation of Health Care Resources – an Ethical Evaluation of the 'QALY' Approach.* (Ashgate Publishing Ltd., 1998)

Mooney David J. and Mikos Antonios G., 'Growing New Organs', *Scientific American* pp 38- 43 (April 1999)

Pedersen, Roger, *Scientific American* (April 1999)

Robertson, John, *Children of Choice,* especially Chapter 2 (Princeton University Press, 1994)

Universal Declaration of Human Rights, Article 16 (1978)

Weinrich, S. L., Pruzan, R., Ma, L. B., Ouellette, M., Tesmer, V. M., Holt, S. E., Bodnar, A. G., Lichtsteiner, S., Kim, N., Thomson, .J A. et al, *Science,* Volume 282 (November 6, 1998)

Weinrich, S. L., Pruzan, R., Ma, L. B., Ouellette, M, Tesmer, V.M., Holt, S. E., Bodnar, A. G., Lichtsteiner, S., Kim, N. W., Trager, J. B., Taylor, R. D , Carlos, R, Andrews, W. H., Wright, W. E., Shay, J. W., Harley, C.B., Morin, G. B., 'Reconstitution of human telomerase with the template RNA component hTR and the catalytic protein subunit hTRT', *Nature Genetics*, Vol.17, No.4, pp.498-502 (1997)

The Right to Die

Dworkin, G., Frey, R.G., Bok, Sissela, *Euthanasia and Physician-Assisted Suicide: for and against* (Cambridge University Press, 1998)

Glover, Jonathan, *Causing Death and Saving Lives* (Harmondsworth: Penguin, 1990)

Uniacke, S. and McCloskey, H .J., 'Peter Singer and Non-Voluntary "Euthanasia": tripping down the slippery slope', *Journal of Applied Philosophy*, 9.2 (1992)

Uniacke, S., 'Was Mary's Death Murder?', *Medical Law Review,* vol 9, no. 3 (2001)

Uniacke, S., 'A Critique of the Preference Utilitarian Objection to Killing People', *Australasian Journal of Philosophy,* vol. 80, no. 2 (2002)

Harming the Dead

Epicurus, *Letter on Happiness* (various translations and editions)

Feldman, Fred, *Confrontations With the Reaper: A Philosophical Study of the Nature and Value of Death* (Oxford University Press, 1994)

Nagel, T., *Mortal Questions* (Cambridge University Press, 1979)

Robinson, Richard, *An Atheist's Values* (Blackwell, 1964, out of print, or http://www.positiveatheism.org/hist/athval0.htm)

Salt, Henry (Eds Hendrick, G. and Hendrick W.), *The Savour of Salt* (Centaur Press, 1989)

Williams, Bernard, *Problems of the Self* (Cambridge University Press, 1976)

The Afterlife

Beauvoir, S. de, *Pour une morale de l'ambiguïté* (Gallimard, 1947)

Beauvoir, S. de and Frechtman, B., *The Ethics of Ambiguity* (Philosophical Library, 1949)

Broad, C. D., *The Mind and its Place in Nature* (Kegan Paul & Co, 1925)

Broad, C. D., *Religion, Philosophy, and Psychical Research; Selected Essays* (Harcourt, Brace, 1953)

Broad, C. D., *Lectures on Psychical Research, incorporating the Perrott lectures given in Cambridge University in 1959 and 1960* (Routledge & Kegan Paul; Humanities Press, 1962)

Flew, A., 'Selves' in *Mind* LVIII(231): 355-358 (1949)

Flew, A., 'Locke and the problem of personal identity' *Philosophy* Vol. XXVI no. 96 pp53-68 (1951)

Flew, A., *A New Approach to Psychical Research* (Watts, 1953)

Flew, A., *The Logic of Mortality* (Blackwell, 1987)

Parfit, D., *Reasons and Persons* (OUP, 1984)

Ryle, G., *The Concept of Mind* (Hutchinson, 1949)

Seth Pringle-Pattison, A., *The Idea of Immortality; the Gifford lectures delivered in the University of Edinburgh in the year 1922* (Clarendon Press, 1922)

Swinburne, R., *The Evolution of the Soul* (Oxford University Press, 1986)